THE STORY OF TOLWORTH

The cover illustration is taken from two sources:

- The Ordnance Survey map of 1816; the first series of these maps to cover the whole of England
- An aerial photograph of Tolworth taken in the late 1960s, after the building of Tolworth Tower

Patricia Ward has lived in the Tolworth and Surbiton area for more than 50 years. She was born and raised in Surrey, attended grammar schools in Guildford and Aldershot and from there went to Girton College, Cambridge, where she read History. Pat was married to David Ward, vicar of St. Paul's, Hook, 1988-93. She is a long-standing member of the Surbiton Historical Society, of the Friends of the Kingston Museum; and is a member of St. George's, her local church in Tolworth She is the author of From Talworth Hamlet to Tolworth Tower, 1975, a history of the Tolworth parish of St. Matthew's, and of a work of research in the history of Godalming.

The current book widens her 1975 work from what was the story of the parish to the story of the whole town, from Domesday to our own time, and looking ahead.

Bob Phillips by profession was a management consultant; he was formerly a Partner in the firm Ernst & Young, North America; co-author of a book on information systems strategy. By training, he was a student of Social and Political Sciences at the University of Cambridge. Bob was one of the founders of the Milton Keynes Forum - a group which lobbies for intelligent city planning, created at the time that the Milton Keynes Development Corporation was prematurely dismantled by Mrs Thatcher's government. Bob Phillips lives on the north side of Tolworth and he is a member of the Friends of the Kingston Museum.

Also by Patricia Ward

From Talworth Hamlet to Tolworth Tower, 1975

THE STORY OF TOLWORTH

by
PATRICIA WARD
with BOB PHILLIPS

published with lulu.com

First published in the United Kingdom in 2015

Broomfield Press

ISBN 978-0-9933487-0-9

THIS BOOK IS DEDICATED

to

The Surbiton and District
Historical Society

2015

CONTENTS

CONTENTS

CONTENTS

THE NAME "TOLWORTH"

The name "Tolworth" has evolved with many variants. In the centuries following the Norman conquest, there are recorded variants such as "Taleorde", Talewurda", "Taleworda" and even "Talasworp". In the Middle Ages, there is "Tolesworth" and "Talworth". The name "Tolworth" emerges rather late - it is the normal usage in the 19th century.

For this book we have chosen simplicity - we use the current name, "Tolworth", throughout. It does mean in the early chapters that we are not using the name(s) that people of the time would have recognised. It seemed to us, though, that it would make the book easier to read if we used the same name throughout.

PREFACE

For those of us, like the authors, lucky enough to live in Tolworth, this book is a celebration of the long history of this little town on the edge of London. It has almost become accepted that Tolworth hardly has a significant history - everyone, including historians, have treated Tolworth, if at all, as an unregarded footnote in the development of Surrey or of London. What this book celebrates, among other things, is that, in early medieval times, Tolworth was a significant place on the map, and we have traced, as far as the records allow, the continuous history of this place.

There has been an interesting transition in this writing. The first six chapters have been the writing of history, but the last chapter, for the principal author of this book, has been as much a matter of remembering. We have also looked forward a little, to speculate on the larger role that Tolworth is taking up in the future of London.

In order to appreciate this story fully, it is important to place it in the wider context of the history of our land. We have endeavoured to make this easier for our readers by providing enough of that context in the notes to the story. Our intention is that the story should be easily readable on its own, and for that reason, we have published the main text as a continuity, separately from the notes, which are all together at the back of the book. We apologise for the indication, in the main text, of references to these notes; we hope this does not distract those who are reading the story uninterrupted.

For those not fortunate enough to live in our town, this story, we believe, offers an illustrative example of the way in which communities develop on the edge of the Metropolis. The shape of the story of Tolworth, and the sources from which we have traced its story, can, we believe, be repeated for many, many communities on the edge of London, and maybe also other great cities, and we commend this as a study well worth pursuing, not only for the value to the communities themselves, but for the contribution it makes to the history of this great city.

The principal author, approximately 40 years ago, produced another book about Tolworth, entitled <u>From Talworth Hamlet to Tolworth Tower</u>. That book's primary focus was on the Tolworth parish of St. Matthew's. The present book's focus is on the town and community, of which the parish is a part, and in this book we draw upon, and extend, some of the history in the earlier volume. Among other things, we have made discoveries in writing the present book, about the history of medieval Talworth that were not known at the time of writing the first book and which have not been published previously. We have also brought forward from that earlier volume, with permission, the delightful drawings by Mary Platford, now sadly deceased.

CHAPTER 1

BEGINNINGS

Tolworth is not a place that people come to seeking things of historical interest. There are no great buildings of major national importance, there is no great art and few of us relate to the individuals who lived here long ago. Thousands of people pass through every day in shiny cars along the A3, the modern fast road which links London and Portsmouth. Some will be on the A240, the road which joins Kingston and Ewell, and meets Stane Street (A29), going on to the Sussex coast and Kent. Tolworth is on the fringe of Greater London, being now part of the Royal Borough of Kingston upon Thames. For most of its long story, it was part of Surrey and in some centuries more involved with Ewell than with Kingston. Although Tolworth seems insignificant in the context of the great affairs of the realm, its story reflects some of the major developments in English history and shows how they moulded the lives of ordinary people over the centuries.

Iron Age settlement

In the vicinity of Kingston there is evidence of settled life from the early stone ages. In the introduction to Shaan Butters' magnificent work <u>That Famous Place</u>, she gives an outline of the prehistoric finds in the area including Malden, Worcester Park, and Tolworth. There is evidence of a small settlement of three round-houses during the middle Iron Age[1] (*circa* 600 BC to 43 AD) in what is Alpine Avenue in 2015. Similarly, in the area of Tolworth Court Farm there was already a settlement in this period. Closed fields appear to have been laid out, and possibly fields for sheep and cattle. By the end of the Iron Age, the land by the Hogsmill River was being profitably farmed.

The name of Tolworth, however, does not appear until the reference in Domesday Book of 1086[2]. Blair suggests that Tolworth is of Saxon origin: "worth" in Anglo-Saxon means an idol or a shrine. He suggests that "Tolworth" is the land of Tol – a person who lived here.[3]

Reconstruction of an Iron Age settlement at New Malden

The Domesday Book records two manors in Tolworth. Both were held from the Crown by Richard, son of Count Gilbert, ancestor of the English house of de Clare, and it records that they were in the Kingston Hundred[4]. The small manor was in the hands of Ralph as Lord of the Manor[5], and seems to have diminished since Saxon

times. The other, larger one, was held from Richard by Picot. Domesday Book records that it had a mill, meadows, 5½ acres and half a rod of land, and 22 peasants. The fact that a mill is mentioned suggests that it would become Tolworth Court Farm – a settlement which was a continuation from the late Iron Age. Both manors were valued at 60 shillings. Later on there seems also to have been a third manor spoken of as South Tolworth Manor. It might have been linked with Ewell.

It has been estimated that the population of the two Manors at the time of the Conquest[6] may have been about 120[7]. It may well have been greater in Saxon times and it would double in the succeeding three centuries.

King Henry I, reigned 1100-1135,
one of the Norman Kings

The Manor of Tolworth

Tout foys prest

Picot

After the Conquest, the tenancy of Tolworth Manor was held directly from the King by the de Clare family as part of their major holding. Richard, son of Count Gilbert (the guardian of William the Conqueror in his childhood) was the first tenant-in-chief. Richard - Sir Richard Fitz Gilbert - was the first to take the de Clare name. By 1086 Domesday records that it is held from them by the Picot family under whom it seems to have flourished[8].. About 1180, the records[9] of St Mary's Convent in Merton[10] tell us that Peter de Tolworth (a member of the Picot family) made a grant to Merton Abbey of all his lands "free from all exactions save to the King".

In their account of the excavation in 2000, the Kingston University Archaeological Society say that Henry Gerard of Guildford held a manor in an area "which fits our area closely" - it may have been South Tolworth Manor or Tolworth Court Farm. He was succeeded by Henry Say, the constable of Guildford Castle. This castle dominated the Surrey countryside and protected the Guildford gap. The constable was undoubtedly a man of power and unquestionable loyalty to the Crown. After his death

Edward II receiving his crown

the manor was kept by Joan, his wife, who had two further husbands.

These two husbands, Herbert de Borhante and then Thomas Corbet, were both involved in the Court of Edward II. In 1320 Thomas Corbet transferred the Tolworth manor to Hugh Despenser the younger[11], the favourite of Edward II at the time. Being situated between the royal palace at Sheen[12] and London, the Despensers entertained the King at Tolworth[13]. After the execution of both Hugh Despenser and his son for treason, the manor passed to Queen Isabella – then widow of Edward II – and her lover Roger Mortimer.

During their tenancy it appears that the Tolworth Manor was flourishing. It is from Isabella that we have a description of the manor house in 1327[14]: "a chief house enclosed by diches. The site contains two halls, with chapel and six chambers, a kitchen with chamber, a bakehouse and brewhouse. It has a gate and a drawbridge. Outside the ditches there are two weirs, two sheds, a building for turning carts and other buildings for cows, a stable and a piggery. There is a garden and a watermill. The jurors say that the mill of Tolworth is Brayest Mulne."[15]

In the summer of 2000 the Kingston University Archaeo-logical Society undertook an excavation to locate the house. This involved a great deal of archaeological labour. Sadly, no relevant remains of the medieval manor were found. Some of the documentary evidence for its existence is quoted in the paper published after the dig.[16]

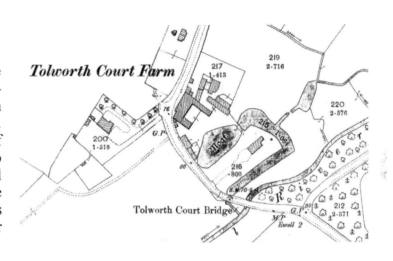

An explanation for the negative findings may be found in the fact explained by Blair[17] that moated manor houses sometimes replaced earlier simpler houses nearby, but on a different site. On the other hand, the remains of Tolworth Manor may be hidden by the A240 road. It is a pity that the manor buildings did not come to light because, in the intervening years, Tolworth has come to be considered as almost a place without a history.

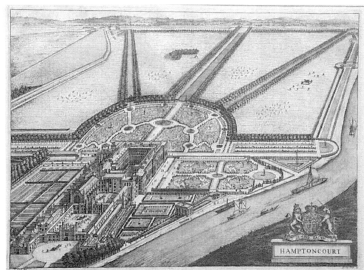

Hampton Court Palace and
Gardens in about 1670

Tolworth Manor was a local court for the area. Documents of 1461 and 1485[18] indicate that Tolworth was the seat of a Baron's Court[19]. It was a tithing of Ewell[20] and part of the Hundred courts which maintained the King's Peace. As such it would hear local cases concerned with road maintenance and land rights. When this arrangement was made is unknown. (Warne, 2014)

Nonsuch Palace in about 1670

Map of Surrey, 1596

Littl...

Salam

Ox

Sunbury

Kingston

Martyn

Mycham

Shepperton

Akecourt
Walton
H.Weridfey

Hampton
Q.Court

IIII

Combe Neuill

Worcdon

Sutton

Walling

Cugfchtton

Wottcott

Oatland

Waybrydge

Efher
E.Mowffey

Thames Diton

Maldon

Chyame

Byflort

St Georges hill

Efher

Chergeworth
Claygate

Long Ditton

Tadworth cort

Kinfud

V

Abroke

Chefington

Ewell

Woodmanfbury

Cobham ftr

Elsham court

Horton

Bauftcd

Cobham

III

Epfcham

Ockham

Stoke Dabernt

Afhtede
Randolls
Letherhead

Wilmtere
ponde

IX

Burghhoue

Ripley

Slyffeld
Fetcham
gr Bockham
Prcfton
Little Bockham

Norbury

Mychelham

Walton

Tadworth

Effregham

E Horfley
W Horfley

Poffton

Hedley

II

On the previous page we reproduce an extract of a map that was made in 1594 by John Norden (published in 1596). The map is reproduced in: <u>250 years of map making in the County of Surrey</u>, a collection of reproductions of printed maps, published between the years 1579-1823 with introductory notes by William Ravenhill', published in 1974 by Harry Margary, Lympne Castle, Kent.

The map indicates how important Tolworth Court must have been in the Middle Ages. It is clearly prominent on the roads between Kingston and Hampton Court, and Nonsuch Palace (although the position of the Manor is slightly misplaced on the map). Its position would also have been important to a traveller from Hampton Court to the summer residence of the Archbishop of Canterbury, at Croydon Palace By way of comparison, note that neither Surbiton nor Norbiton feature on this map.

It is clear from this map that Tolworth's part in history was not negligible in mediaeval times, even if it sank somewhat into obscurity later.

Croydon Palace later, about 1760

Daily life for Tolworth people

Life for the people of Tolworth during the Middle Ages was that of a peasant community living and working in in the vicinity of a manor. The records of Domesday shows that there may have been five cottages in each manor with an addition of say 10 people occupying the manor house. Each cottage would have a virgate (holding) of 13 acres, not usually in one piece.

The tenant would use the land to grow food for his family, taking any surplus to the market in Kingston. He would also keep cattle and pigs. The heavy London clay was more suitable for dairy than for arable farming. The "virgate" was a measurement of service to the Lord of the Manor, but was frequently commuted in part to rent. As well as this, a tenant would enjoy rights to use the common.

It is difficult to imagine that all the area now under tarmac, bricks and mortar and garden fences was, until the 20th century, land which joined the commons of Kingston, Surbiton, Malden and Chessington. We must not think of common land as wasteland. It was of great significance to the life of the peasants, providing wood for fires, for building and for making of furniture and tools. It also gave rabbits for the pot, pannage[21] for the pigs to forage, and wild fruit and herbs for food and medicine. The River similarly was important: for travel to Kingston and Ewell as well as for fish for the table and for rushes used in building and to make candle lights.

By the standards of medieval living, Tolworth was reasonably prosperous. The land was fertile. We know for instance that in the 12th century, merchants from London were buying land in the parish of Cuddington[22] next to Tolworth. In the light of the scant surviving documents it is easy to assume that Tolworth was a manor of no importance. Further consideration of the little we know suggests that this is not true. In fact the Tolworth Court Manor remained a significant manor in the North Surrey/London areas, as the map on page 8 indicates. Moreover, it is reasonable to assume from the social status of the Lords of the Manor and the description of the house in 1327[23] that the Tolworth Court Manor was regarded as substantial and was probably a significant place.

Later on in the 14th century the manor house seems to have fallen into disrepair, especially after the Black Death[24]. This was common for many manors across England. In later centuries the house became an ordinary farmhouse and agriculture continued until recent times.

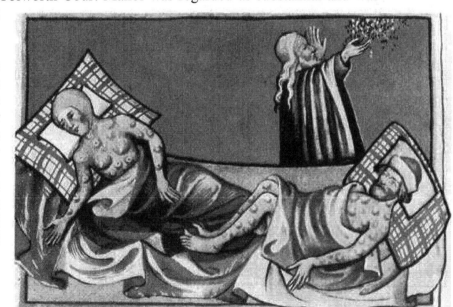

The Church in Tolworth and Long Ditton

Domesday Book does not report the existence of any church in Tolworth. It does mention one in Long Ditton. As Picot held both settlements from Richard, son of Count Gilbert, this was presumably regarded as adequate. In fact for many centuries Tolworth was described as "a hamlet in the parish of Long Ditton". It was never part of the large parish of Kingston, which was the Minster church for the Kingston Hundred[25].

The concept of parishes as land and as people in the care of a particular priest does not develop until the mid-12th century[26]. Churches were built at the convenience and expense of the Lord of the Manor. Possibly the one mentioned in Domesday was a Saxon wooden church replaced by a Norman stone one. A 12th century wall still exists as the base of a wall in the Memorial Garden of St Mary's Church, Long Ditton.

Although Long Ditton church was not ever under the care of Kingston, the Priory of St Mary in Merton would soon effectively be its superior. The Priory had been founded by Henry I in 1117, and was of Augustinian foundation[27]. This meant that it provided not just the usual community life but also took a lively interest in any parish churches connected to it. We know that shortly before 1180 Peter de Tolworth gave the advowson (the right to choose priests and take some of the tithe) to the Priory[28]. It is interesting to note that his neighbour Eudes de Malden did the same for the church at Malden (now Old Malden).

12th century arch from Merton Priory

The name "Peter" suggests his Norman descent; he was of the Picot family, who would have been supportive of the religious revival[29] of the 11th to 12th century. He was also, it seems, a wealthy man and held land outside Tolworth. It is on record that at about 1160 he surrendered the rights over the church at Horne[30], a manor south of Bletchingley, to the Priory at Lewes[31]. It seems that Horne was originally part of Bletchingley but that perhaps its church had been built by some Lord in the intervening years and it was being reclaimed, as the church at Bletchingley had been taken over by Lewes Priory. Be that as it may, this incident reveals that Peter de Tolworth was, for a knight of the mid 12th century, a man of considerable wealth and determination.

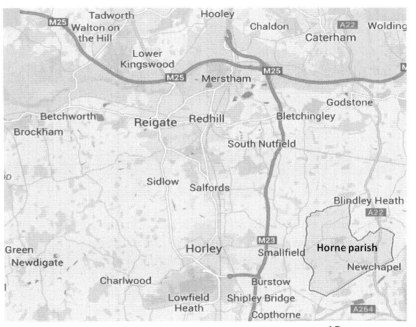

After handing over the advowson of Long Ditton Church to St Mary's Priory he personally entered the monastery and took vows as a monk[32]. Eudes de Malden entered the Priory at the same time. Peter de Tolworth is mentioned in the Priory records[33]

Tolworth was nonetheless without a parish church of its own and remained as a "hamlet in the parish of Long Ditton" until the building of St Matthew's in 1875.

It seems, however, that with the rebuilding of Tolworth Court in the 13th century a chapel was included[34]. Perhaps this was an indication of the growing significance of Tolworth.

In considering the life of Tolworth during the period 1066 to 1501 one must feel a little sad that the evidence is so tantalisingly scarce. The map of 1596 showing Talworth Court as a significant place in the centre of North Surrey must confirm, however, that at the time it was well-known. One can only hope that further documentation will be discovered.

CHAPTER 2

TOLWORTH SINCE THE TUDORS AND STUARTS

The Black Death in the 1340s and 50s greatly weakened the feudal system of land tenure[35] which had existed in England since 1066 (or even before). It was, however, the changes in the Church – the Reformation[36] – which finally killed it off. After the Wars of the Roses, at the Battle of Bosworth in 1485, Henry VII and the Tudor family secured the English throne. His son, Henry VIII, saw the importance of establishing a secure line of succession, and therefore needed a male heir. He also needed money. He broke with Rome and by an Act of Parliament made himself Head of the Church in England.

With Thomas Cromwell as his henchman, and a subservient Parliament to pass the Act of Supremacy (1534), Henry was enabled to seize the lands held by monastic institutions and to dissolve them[37]. For Tolworth this meant that the Priory of St Mary's, Merton, which had played such a large part in the life of the area, was dissolved and the land, including the manor and its holdings, reverted to the Crown.

We know that the first person to own Tolworth after the Dissolution was a courtier named David Vincent[38]. He was a gentleman of the bedchamber to the King and would, therefore, have been on personal terms with Henry. Whether he bought Tolworth or was given it for services rendered we do not know, but his property was passed in 1565 to his son Thomas Vincent on his death.

Two years later in 1567, the whole estate (which included Long Ditton) was sold to George Evelyn[39], who was already a substantial land owner in Surrey, and it remained in that family until 1692. The Evelyns were a lively and gifted family. Locally, George Evelyn's main significance was that he developed the manufacture of gunpowder on the Hogsmill River, together with a similar development in Godstone, under royal letters patent in 1589. These projects produced a fortune for the family.

The young John Evelyn

The Evelyn family made a significant contribution to the nation in the seventeenth century. John Evelyn (1620-1706) was a member of the Royal Society, promoting scientific studies on such subjects as air pollution in London and the provision of sufficient wood for the Navy. His best-known endeavour was the writing of his diary reflecting life in London in the 1660s – much like the diary written by his friend and contemporary, Samuel Pepys.

In 1692 Tolworth became the property of Sir Joseph Allston who held it until 1723 when it became the property of Sir Stephen Glynn. The trustees of a James Scawen were the next people to hold Tolworth.

In 1781, Tolworth was bought by Nathaniel Polhill[40]. He was a wealthy man who had made his money as a tobacco merchant. He was the Member of Parliament for Southwark. The family also owned Howberry Hall in Bedfordshire and lands in Surrey including Heathfield, Mayfield and Burwash. In the three centuries which followed the Dissolution of the Monasteries, Tolworth had been in the hands of wealthy city men who never lived in the community as the Lords of the Manor had done, and it is notable that they left no mark such as building a fine house. They seem to have had no interest in agriculture either, so that Tolworth and its few inhabitants appear to have carried on undisturbed by the new methods of farming which were being practised elsewhere in England.

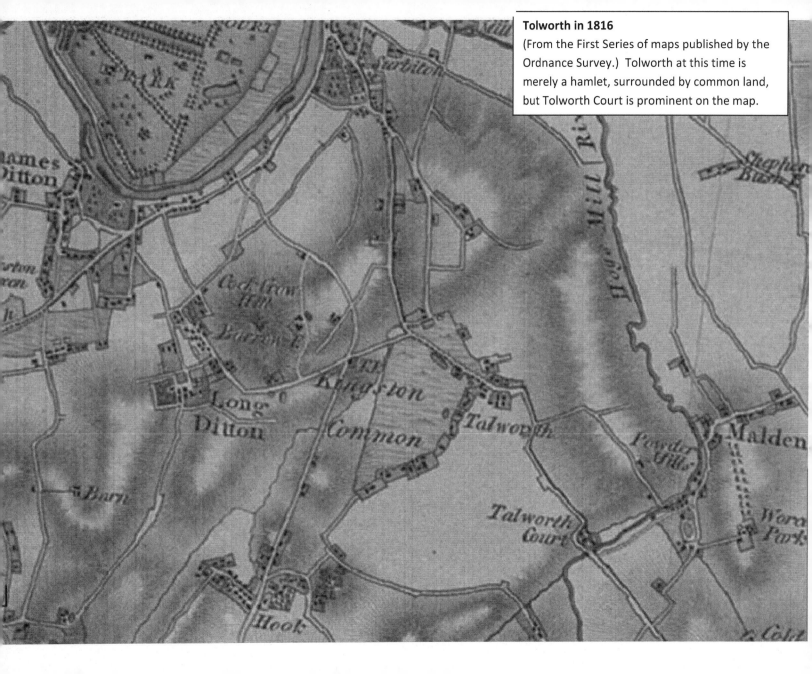

Tolworth in 1816
(From the First Series of maps published by the Ordnance Survey.) Tolworth at this time is merely a hamlet, surrounded by common land, but Tolworth Court is prominent on the map.

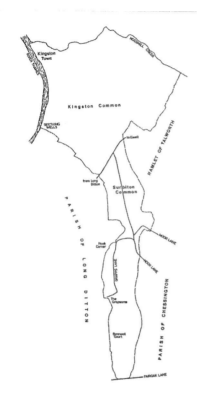

The hamlet of Tolworth

It must be appreciated that at no time can Tolworth be called a village. By the 18th century Tolworth Court Farm together with Holland's Farm and Neal's Farm, on either side of the Ewell Road, were tenanted farm houses, with farmland. We know that there was also by 1718 an alehouse because Thomas Mills was prosecuted at the quarter-sessions for keeping a disorderly house[41]. But Tolworth had no large or memorable house and was still a part of the Long Ditton parish although it was separated from the Church by a strip of land belonging to Kingston parish (as it always had been — shown on the map here).

Most of the land of Tolworth was common[42] — a common which merged into the Chessington, Kingston, Malden and Surbiton Commons. The first census return which we have for Tolworth gives the number of inhabitants in 1821 as 234 — a figure not unlike the one estimated for the area in Norman times. We have a description of the Tolworth Court Farm: by the beginning of the 19th century it was no longer a Court but an ordinary tenanted farm.

This description is in a document dated 1806, but contains a description of the Tolworth Court Farm copied from a document of 1723[43]. We read that the farm consisted of the manor house with 10 cottages, 10 stables, and gardens. 400 acres of land was being cultivated with 50 acres of pasture. A survey conducted by the Government Surveyor in 1803[44] showed Tolworth Court Farm was worth £222-2-9d.

At the same time Neal's Farm was worth £81-1-9d and Holland's Farm £97-3-5d.

The record of 1841 concerning the tax for the upkeep of the main road[45] shows that there were two public houses, namely the Red Lion and the Royal Oak, a dairy man called Filbrook, two farmers, Hipwell and Smith, and a smithy and a farrier. These people would have lived in the area where the Red Lion Road meets the main Ewell Road.

The main road (on the line of what is now the A240) was the most significant feature in Tolworth from the 16th to the 18th centuries. In Tudor times it had been the main route from Hampton Court[46] to Nonsuch Palace[47]; passing through the main hunting ground of Henry VIII. We know that Parliament in the 17th century had made a grant for the upkeep of this road[48]. In 1764 local citizens were taxed to pay for the repair of the road.

A Post Office Directory of 1845 lists two public houses, the Red Lion and the Royal Oak, two farmers named Hipwell and Smith, a brickmaker, Gribble, a carpenter, a blacksmith and a farrier. In the Parliamentary electoral lists before 1867, only the names of Mr Hipwell and Mr Smith are mentioned. The pre-1867 list is revealing because it names only middle-class male votes.

An ACT for Dividing and Inclosing certain Common Fields in the Hamlet of Shipton, *in the Parish of* Winslow, *in the County of* Bucks.

Example showing an earlier Enclosure Act – this is from another area, not Tolworth

The Tolworth enclosure.

The Tolworth Enclosure Act[49] came very late, in 1820. There is a possible explanation for this: it may be because, since the time of Henry VIII, Tolworth had been the property of absentees, whose interests lay in the City rather than in farming for profit.

During the feudal period land had been held by individuals not as one contained area but as strips scattered over the whole estate. Of course this had been modified in practice from time to time over the centuries because it was very inefficient. With the rise of the population and the coming of industrial towns there was a need for greater productivity in the production of food. Subsistence farming was inadequate. Consequently, there was a general movement across the country to enclose and consolidate each farmer's land as one area which could be more easily and economically cultivated.

The process by which enclosure could take place was carefully orchestrated[50]. Firstly an Act of Parliament was needed, stating the parishes in which enclosure was desired. This would be promoted by an individual or a group with an interest, Nathaniel Polhill in this case. A Surveyor was appointed. For Tolworth it was John Raine, who would oversee and supervise the enclosure and make the award of lands. Some of the land was sold to meet the costs of the operation and the rest would be reallocated giving suitable areas, each in a single piece, to people already holding land.

Inevitably, it was the Lord of the Manor who received the lion's share, namely Nathaniel Polhill; although John Taylor, Peter Lionel King and J. Palmer gained worthwhile holdings. The Polhill acquisitions included not only agricultural land but also usable Commons and the house of Tolworth Court Farm, which was on a long lease. The other significant gainer was Sarah Langley who was awarded land to the north-west of Tolworth in what is now the Southborough Estate. The enclosure documents also described the bridleways and roads which were the responsibility of the community. The names of individuals and the amount that each was to pay was recorded in the Highway Rate Book.

It seems that the Commissioner had some difficulty in deciding where the boundary of Tolworth actually lay. In a document describing the perambulation of the boundary[51] we can see his problem. The Common which formed the main part of the land had never been cultivated, and it joined the Commons of Kingston and

Chessington, with no clear distinction between the Commons. So the boundary was hard to define reliably. During the Kingston enclosure which preceded the Tolworth one, a dispute had arisen. The Commissioner, using a customary procedure, took two older men to the area of the dispute. The party approached the boundary with Kingston which was under dispute.

The party consisted of the Surveyor Raine and several elderly men. One of the group - John Neale - came forward saying that, as a child, he was bumped against a particular tree which was still remaining. John Taylor (aged 89) confirmed that he, when he was 10 or 11 years, had similarly been "bumped" for Mr Scawen, the proprietor of the Tolworth Estate. J. Raine wrote to the owner, Nathaniel Polhill, stating that with these witnesses' evidence Tolworth's claims for the stretch was greater than Kingston's. Surely this must open our eyes to the rural character of Tolworth in the first decade of the 19th century. For the ordinary inhabitant of Tolworth little had changed since medieval times. But ... change was on the way.

Beating the Bounds

CHAPTER 3

THE VICTORIAN AGE - ST MATTHEW'S

The event that triggered the big change of the Victorian era in Tolworth was the building of the Parish Church of St. Matthew's. Strictly speaking, the Church building was not in Tolworth but on land administered by the Surbiton Improvement Commission. The land was donated by a Mr. Curling of Hyde Park who had bought it, after the recent enclosure, from the Langley family. The Church and Vicarage were built at the sole expense of William Matthew Coulthurst – a donation of some £24,000[52]. The background to this most generous act reveals much about the immense wealth and the religious life of the middle years of the 19th century. The story is a complex one.

In the 1830s the London to Southampton Railway company was planning to build a new railway line into the Metropolis. They intended to have a station near Kingston town centre, linking it southward to Woking and the Coast and to Wimbledon, Clapham, Vauxhall and ultimately Waterloo to the north.

The significant citizens of Kingston were divided in response to the proposal[53]. Consequently a second suggestion was made which took the railway line away from the town centre and through a cutting to Surbiton. This was acceptable to the Company and to the landowners. An Act of Parliament allowing for this cutting was passed in 1834.

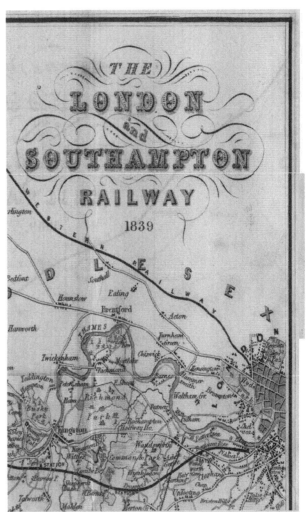

The station, in Surbiton but called Kingston-on-the-Railway, opened in 1838. In the January of that year a farmer, Christopher Terry, who held Maple Farm in Surbiton, died. He also owned land on Surbiton Hill. In his will he had expressly stated that his property should be sold by auction on his death.

A certain Thomas Pooley, who lived locally, recognised the impact that the station would have on the value of this land for development. He acquired Maple Farm at a very cheap price. Pooley saw the possibility of developing the area as one of elegance for wealthy commuters travelling daily to the city. In order to achieve his aim, Mr Pooley borrowed £16,000 from Coutts Bank. However, sadly, this was not enough to complete the project and when he asked for a further loan it was refused.

The first Kingston-on-the-Railway station was built by the railway company in the cutting they had to make for the changed, non-Kingston, route.

"There has been no unnecessary expense in architectural designs or decorations, the object aimed at having utility and durability at the smallest possible cost," said the company, describing its station in a report presented at the half-yearly meeting of shareholders in February, 1839. It was a policy that was to enrage passengers for the rest of the century.' [Sampson, page 31]

Pooley also saw the limitations of this narrow view. He persuaded the railway company to move the station to a more convenient location, by giving them a site. Then he built what the Times described as a "very respectable edifice".

(Pooley's vision served future generations well. The station was rebuilt several times on that site, central to the town plan of Surbiton, and it was renamed as many times: Kingston Junction in late 1852, Surbiton and Kingston in 1863, and now Surbiton Station, designed in 1937 by J Robb Scott in the 'International' style.)

One may well ask why the money for such a forward-looking development was not forthcoming. There is evidence that the jealousy of wealthy Kingston Councillors and their interference is one cause. The realisation by Coutts Bank of the value of such an investment and the wealth it would produce in the future may also have played some part. But the upshot was that Thomas Pooley was bankrupted, and Coutts Bank took

over the Surbiton project – and its profits. It seems that the manner by which Coutts acquired this holding of what turned out to be a very valuable investment was remarkably ruthless.[54]

In the eyes of the partners of Coutts Bank in Fleet Street in London, the development of Surbiton must have been a source of interest and discussion. Coutts was a private bank serving people of distinction and wealth, including Queen Victoria. The venture taken from Pooley was the first speculative investment the bank had made in the 150 years since it was founded[55]. Coutts benefitted spectacularly from the growth of Pooley's commuter town.

The rise in the population of the district is reflected in the Surrey Comet of 1874 which reports that the rise in population in the district was prompting the wardens of Long Ditton to consider adding to the size of their church because of the demands. In fact a new church was built in Long Ditton in 1880.

It is revealing that it was Coutts Bank which promoted the bill to set up the Surbiton Improvement Commission in 1855, taking the wealth of Surbiton out of the domain of the Kingston Councillors.

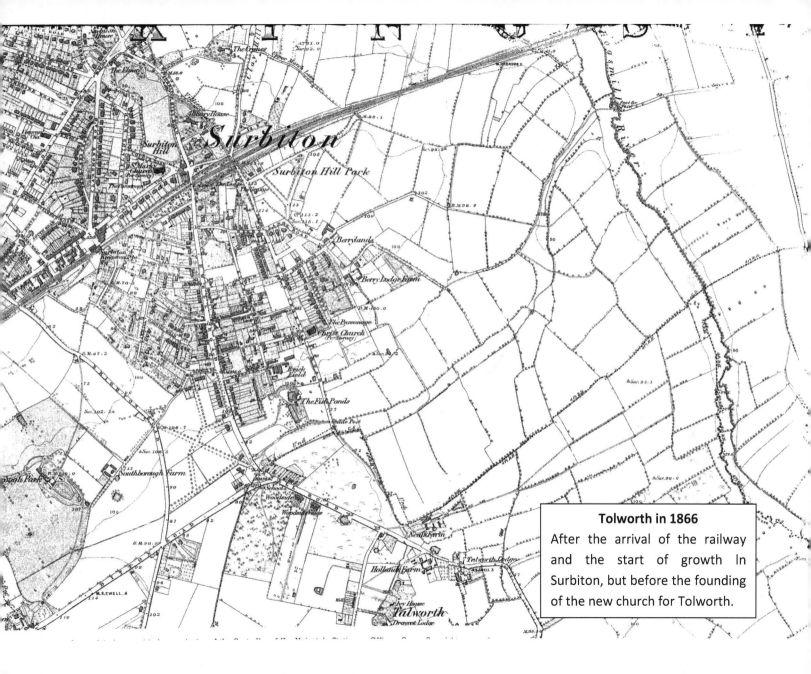

Tolworth in 1866
After the arrival of the railway and the start of growth In Surbiton, but before the founding of the new church for Tolworth.

William Coulthurst, was the Senior Partner in the Bank as the Surbiton project matured. The Coulthurst family had come from Gargrave in Yorkshire, and were solicitors, and he worked at the firm of Ferrar & Co. When an opening arose for William to leave the solicitors' firm and move, in 1827, to a partnership at Coutts, he took the opportunity and remained there for the rest of his working life. He was a Partner in 1842, when the business with Pooley happened, and he was still a Partner - the Senior Partner - in 1875, when St. Matthew's was founded.

In 1836 Coulthurst had moved with his brothers Henry and Nicolas to live at Streatham Lodge with their mother Margaret and their younger sister Mabella. All his life William had been a devout churchman[56] and was very interested in the building of Immanuel; constructed in 1859 out of the parish of St. Leonard's, Streatham, to serve the increase in population in the area around the Common.

Immanuel differed from St. Leonard's in that it was Evangelical in its way of worship and in its theology. The large stone building on the high road overlooking Streatham Common would be filled to offer the worship of the Book of Common Prayer and would be instructed by biblical sermons by the Rev. Eardley. Some of the congregation would come in their carriages; the servants of the households would be expected to attend worship at another church, St. Andrew's, built for their use.

33

The tower remains of Victorian Immanuel Church

The Clapham Sect

As one considers the life of these wealthy people one cannot help feeling that they may well have been influenced by the Clapham Sect who had worshipped at Holy Trinity Church, Clapham Common, earlier in the century. That congregation included William Wilberforce and Hannah More, and were devout people given to social reform and the preaching of a simple gospel message[57]. Immanuel Church, at its foundation, seems also to have reflected this Evangelism, unlike the parish from which it was carved, St. Leonard's.

One can easily speculate on some of the things that would have prompted William Matthew Coulthurst, as an old man, to make such an amazing gift to Tolworth – £24,000 to build St Matthew's Church and Vicarage. His professional life at the Bank had introduced him to the development of the area. His own local interest indicated the growing need. His personal wealth enabled him to make this provision. (Even

The plaque at St. Matthew's Church

after this provision, his estate when he died was £500,000.) He wished to make a suitable memorial to his sister Mabella (who had already died). Moreover, he was a very convinced Evangelical and, like Immanuel, Streatham, St Matthew's was built to display the Evangelical style of worship and social concerns.

One can also speculate that there would have been an element for him, and possibly also for the proprietor of the Bank, Angela Burdett Coutts, of atoning for wrong done in Surbiton 33 years earlier.

It is not difficult to imagine Coulthurst discussing the development of Surbiton with Angela Burdett Coutts: a major partner in the Bank, one of the wealthiest ladies in London, a very prominent philanthropist, friend of Queen Victoria and a pillar of the Church of England.

We know too that with Marjoribanks, a fellow partner, Coulthurst had bought land in Surbiton[58], now Avenue Elmers. He would therefore have been well aware of the development of the district.

These four strands - Evangelical charity, the memory of his sister, knowledge of Surbiton, and atoning for past wrongs may all contribute to the explanation of the extraordinary fact of one man, from way outside the parish, putting up such an enormous sum single-handed to found St. Matthew's.

Description of St Matthew's

The site of St Matthew's is on the southern edge of the land administered by the Surbiton Improvement Commissioners, close to the hamlet of Tolworth (which had always been a part of Long Ditton parish).

Architecturally, it is a pleasing example of a Victorian church in the early English style. The builder was Manley and Rogers of Regent Street. Visually the church dominated the area by the height of its nave (64 feet) and the elegant spire (170 feet) which surmounted it. Richardson, in his book <u>Surbiton, Thirty-two years of self-government</u>, remarked that the Church would hold 800 people.

The walls of Kentish rag-stone were dressed with Bath-stone externally, and faced with yellow brick internally. Black and white marble paved the semicircular apse. A visitor to the new church would have been greatly impressed by its spaciousness and by the light flooding through the clear glass windows of the nave and clerestory. The

tracery which surrounded the windows would have brought to mind the style and colours of the Pre-Raphaelite painters.

We know that Millais and Holman Hunt stayed in Tolworth for about six months in 1851 and that Millais' picture of "Ophelia"[59] was painted on the bank of the Hogsmill River in the six-acre meadow, south of Tolworth.

37

Sponsorship of the new church came from a group of Trustees who had helped with its planning and construction, and who would offer the Vicar support in the early months of its life. The Trustees were: the Rev. E. Garbett, Vicar of Christ Church, Surbiton; two of his leading lay-men: Mr. Strachan and Mr. Stringer; Mr Edmund Coulthurst, the founder's nephew; and the Suffragan Bishop of Guildford. The man appointed as the first vicar was the Rev. T.C. Griffiths. He had been the curate at Immanuel, Streatham and was the founder's nominee; he proved to be a person of energy and leadership and served the parish from 1875 until 1902. The consecration took place on 21 September 1875. At the lunch after the service the High Sheriff of Surrey proposed a toast to William Coulthurst. In replying, Coulthurst said that he wanted to build a church which would last a very long time. The services should be simple and the teaching that of Christ. A comment was made by the Vicar of Christ Church, Surbiton, that they would be obliged to build villas in order to find a congregation for St Matthew's.

Rev. T.C. Griffiths

The parish was created by Orders in Council[60] in 1876. Firstly there was a square of land, bordered by Langley Road, Upper Brighton Road, Ditton Road and Ewell Road, surrendered to the new parish from the Christ Church parish . This area was part of the land under the Surbiton Improvement Commissioners[61] – it was not part of Tolworth. Secondly, there was the hamlet of Tolworth, comprising largely common with a small settlement and farms, as well as Tolworth Court which was surrendered by St Mary's, Long Ditton. This area given by St Mary's to the new parish was to become increasingly significant as the next century rolled on.

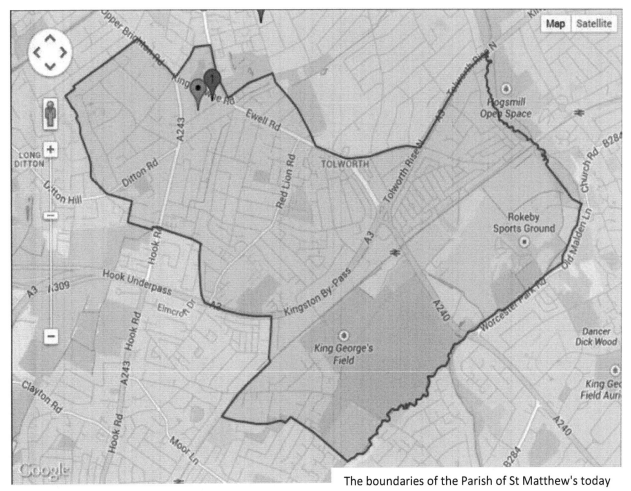

The boundaries of the Parish of St Matthew's today

CHAPTER 4

LIFE IN THE NEW PARISH

By the beginning of 1876, the stone masons had completed their task and the parish boundaries had been set. The first incumbent – the Rev. T.C. Griffiths – had moved from Streatham, where he had been a curate, to become the Vicar of St Matthew's. Griffiths was a Welshman, with a flowing beard and an eloquent style of preaching. Perhaps his origins explain why a paid choir, with organist, was the first addition to the services. In the first six months of the life of the new church an organ blower and bellringers were also employed.

Until April 1876, the Trustees were legally in charge of the Church, but in April 1876 a Vestry meeting[62] was held, and the first two Churchwardens were appointed. The two men were Francis S. Clayton and William Hipwell. Francis Clayton was a local solicitor who lived in a beautiful mansion "Haycroft" which stood back from the Hook Road. He had worshipped at St Pauls, Hook[63], and his main interest was in the promotion of education for children and adults. William Hipwell, on the other hand, was a farmer, tenant to the Lord Egmont, who had bought the Tolworth Manor from Nathaniel Polhill after the enclosure.

Before the founding of St Matthew's, William Hipwell had worshipped at St Mary's, Long Ditton and had been a Churchwarden there. The Hipwell family had been an established element of life in Tolworth over two centuries. William, in the late 19th century, was the major tenant farmer holding up to 500 acres from Lord Egmont. This land included the four farms in Tolworth as well as Berrylands. Although there was some arable land, the main activity was dairy farming (thanks to the damp clay soil).

Evidence of Mr. Hipwell's concern for those who worked for him can still be seen on the frontage of a row of cottages in Red Lion Road with the plaque saying "WH 1867". These houses are still occupied and compare well with houses built a century later. Hipwell's social significance can be seen from the fact that he is one of the only two voters on the pre-1867 Electoral register – the other being Mr. Smith, who at the time tenanted Neal's Farm.

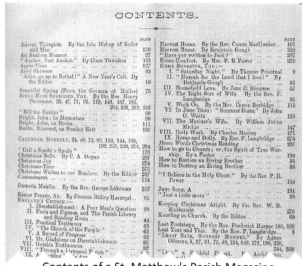

Contents of a St. Matthew's Parish Magazine

Social outreach.

The opening of the new Church was not just a sign of religious activity, it was the beginning of social provision. Just as Immanuel had reached out into the life of the local people, so did St Matthew's. Anyone who reads the parish magazines of the 1880s, which appeared monthly, must be impressed by the energy and versatility of the people, no doubt led by their enthusiastic Vicar and the two Churchwardens. The Parish Magazines[64] of 1883, for example, advertise a performance of the Messiah in February and note that the Night School (which would be teaching adults) was well attended. They note that there had been a discussion on the question of keeping the night school open during the summer months. The reason for this was that it would encourage workers in the local brickfield and navvies on the new railway to attend. There was also a penny bank and a clothing club. In June, a sermon was preached in behalf of the Girls Friendly Society. There were open air Evangelical services during the summer months, and Temperance meetings, with piano concerts. The Church Missionary Society[65], which had been formed in 1799 by the Clapham Sect to evangelise the British colonies in Africa, was enthusiastically supported. Pictures of the Africans appear in the magazine. In December 1883 a sale of work in aid of the Church Missionary Society was held in the Vicarage and it is interesting to note that similar events were held yearly until 1990. Such activities brought new width to the lives of people living in rural Tolworth. They also reflected the interests of the Church of Immanuel from which William Coulthurst and Rev. Griffiths had come.

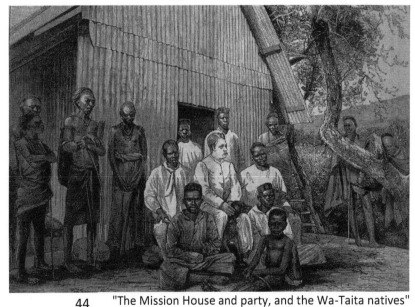

44   "The Mission House and party, and the Wa-Taita natives"

St. Matthew's School.

The growing demands of commerce and industry for workers who were educated in basic skills meant that there was a need for a parish school. Elementary education was provided by two voluntary societies: the National Society, under the auspices of the Church of England; and the British and National Society, which was supported by other denominations. Where neither of these offered satisfactory provision, then a School Board would be appointed for the area. The School Board had powers to raise a rate and to provide schools with non-denominational Bible teaching. It was probably fear of the parish school being constituted as a Board

45

School that impelled the congregation of St. Matthew's to address so speedily the issue of providing a school.

In June 1878 a bazaar was held in the gardens of Mr Eglington to raise money for the school, with stalls and entertainment from the local brass band. A sum of £315-13-1d was raised (the equivalent in 2014 would be around £200,000). The original school buildings consisted of two rooms: one for the infants (22' x 15') and the other for the older children (50' x 22'). This was considered to be adequate for 170 children. The weekly cost to the older children was 3d a week and for the infants 2d. Elementary education was neither free nor compulsory. In September 1882 the attendance was 62 on average.

A 2013 photograph of the first St. Matthew's school building

School fees were not the only source of income. The local School Board of Managers also requested a Parliamentary grant. Inspectors were sent to schools to report on their achievements, on the poverty of the locality and, where appropriate, to award merit grants. The reports of the Inspectors and the school's own log book are very revealing of Tolworth. At the opening of St Matthew's school in January 1881, work began with Miss Berry as Headmistress. An examination was held and the children were found "very backward". In 1882, the Inspectors' Report said: "a better state of discipline will no doubt be achieved as the children get used to the school". In 1883, a Merit Grant was given for progress, but this does not seem to have been maintained and the money was reduced. A manager's meeting was held and Miss Berry resigned.

Her place was taken by Miss Chilcott, who was more of a disciplinarian. The Inspectors noted in 1886: "The children are far more orderly than usual and are in course of being cured of their habit of chatting under examination". The infants did not receive a good report; described as "dull, ignorant and rather restless". Consequently the infant grant was reduced and infant teacher Miss Brooker left the school.

It must be acknowledged that the establishing of elementary education was no easy matter. This was for most rural families the first generation of schooling and many of their parents would have been illiterate. There were many reasons why attendance was often interrupted: bad weather, outbreaks of fever in the area, or, one day, rumours that the children were to be vaccinated at school. The school would close for bazaars and, of course, for Derby Day. However, as the school settled into the life of Tolworth one must feel that St Matthew's was making a major contribution to the community.

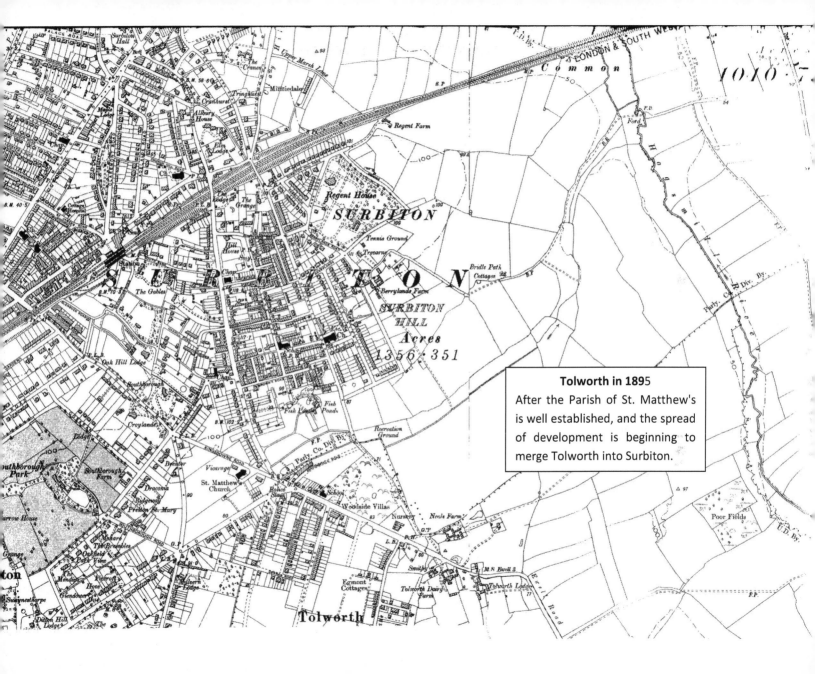

Tolworth in 1895
After the Parish of St. Matthew's is well established, and the spread of development is beginning to merge Tolworth into Surbiton.

By the 1880s there was the beginning of building in the Red Lion Road area. Under Captain Cundy, the new Churchwarden, it was decided to build a Mission Hall in Pyne Road. The purpose of the Hall was to provide a place for Evangelical services, mothers meetings, and Bible studies. Capt. Cundy was particularly keen on promoting the Temperance Society, and to this end concerts and talks were arranged. The Hall also provided a reading room and library for local people. In August 1885, the annual exhibition of fruit, flowers and vegetables grown in cottage gardens took place. They were judged by Mr Eglington's gardener. It is easy to dismiss the work of small halls like the one in Pyne Road but at their time they drew people together and lifted their horizons.

The location of the old Mission Hall on Pyne Road

Pyne Road today - an interesting contrast of the modern tower in the background, a coal merchant's premises that was founded in 1898 (W.E. Crockers Ltd) in the foreground and the site of the old Mission Hall in between. The Fever Hospital / Tolworth Hospital is located to the right, one street south of Pyne Road.

CHAPTER 5

FROM HAMLET TO SUBURB

The coming of St Matthew's Church in 1875 was undoubtedly a major event in the story of Tolworth. It provided a focus, in the form of a beautiful building for the area. But it also made a meeting place for leaders of the emerging society. Perhaps it was this that made them aware of the needs of Tolworth and of their own responsibilities. Hence the many activities of the early 1880s.

But it must be admitted that by the 1880s the area was developing economically, so that neither the church nor voluntary work by philanthropic citizens could meet the demands. The next 20 years – 1891 to 1911 – would see economic growth, the rise of population and the emergence of a suburban environment.

The population growth of Tolworth is shown in the census returns. The first census we have with Tolworth independent of Long Ditton was in 1821, about the same time as the enclosures, and it registers a population of 234. This is not very different from the figure which it is assumed would have lived in Tolworth at the time of Domesday.

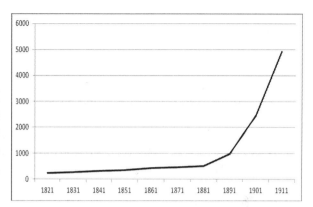

In 1831, the population was 264 and in 1841 317. By 1871 the figure had grown to 464 and was still only 508 in 1881. It was not until the 1880s that there was a significant leap in the growth of Tolworth's population as shown in the census. The 1891 figure was 979. Subsequently, this figure would continue to grow exponentially.

The nature of the change during the period 1851-1881 has been carefully researched by Brian Hawksbee. In his study Tolworth: Population and Development, an analysis of the census returns from this period, he shows a relative decline in the number of heads of households involved in agriculture from 68.5% in 1851 to 33.6% in 1881. The same census returns reveal that in 1851 19% of the workforce was in domestic service. By 1881, this figure has risen to 30%. It seems likely that most of the rise in population figures can be accounted for by the erection of substantial middle-class housing on the Ewell Road. The census returns show that by 1861, a barrister and a professor of chemistry lived in Tolworth. The 1881 census gives a much fuller list of occupations followed by the heads of households in Tolworth. These included baker, bailiff, cattle salesman, florist, missioner, merchant, paper hanger and tailor. Such a growing list of professions and trades indicates that by the early 1880s the social composition of Tolworth was becoming more complex and varied. It even included a well-known naturalist, Richard Jefferies, who lived in the late 70s at Woodside on the Ewell Road. Bear in mind that until the 1880s Tolworth was largely common land with four farms of which the most important was Tolworth Court Farm. There was a public house, a smithy, and a handful of houses in the Ewell Road near the boundary of the Surbiton Improvement Commission area, and the Hipwell cottages. This is shown in the ordnance survey map of 1866 (see page 32).

When we consider the reasons for the escalation of the population, one major source is the development of brick-making in Red Lion Road. The 1881 census shows 10 workers in the brickfields. The clay soil, which had provided the lush pastures for the cattle, became the basis for local industry. Kelly's directory of 1882 gives Cusk and Co. of Red Lion House as brick-maker and also mentions Spence Sawyer as a "farmer and brickmaker". There was a brickyard on Fullers' farmland, now the location of the playing fields of the Tolworth Girls School, at the end of Red Lion Road, close by the by-pass.

Another development encouraging population growth was the breakup of the Southborough Estate. In 1882 the first of a

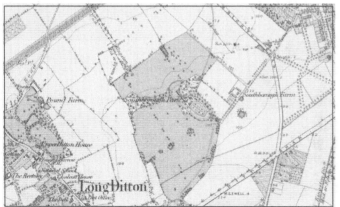

The Southborough Estate and environs in 1867

53

series of auctions was advertised in the Surrey Comet. It was held by the National Liberal Land Corporation, of 40 Charing Cross Road. Plots suitable for villas to be in Ellerton and Ditton Roads were offered. They were described as "beautifully wooded with fir trees". They were near the station (Surbiton), of "liberal depth and with excellent water supply". There were sound roads with kerbed paths. In May, a similar auction was advertised for June 22nd with plots, free conveyancing and tithe rent redemption of 10%[66] payable at auction by the purchaser. This marked the end of the Langley family's estate. Southborough Lodge was bought by Capt. James Cundy in September 1883. In the Surrey Comet, residents complained "there are very few parishioners who would not view with dismay the sale of Southborough Park" and went on to suggest that the Southborough Park be bought for open space.

The Surrey Comet in February 1881 also reported that land was being sold to developers in Red Lion Road. Charles Butler sold 3 acres as "gentlemen's residences" or as building plots. William Hipwell sold 10 substantially built houses let to weekly tenants. The paper remarked "there is a great demand in the area which is considered healthy."

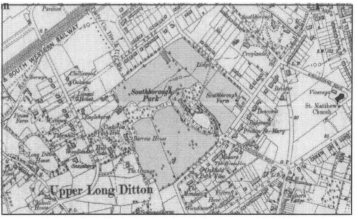

The Southborough Estate and environs in 1895

Tolworth Isolation Hospital

By the time of the 1870s, the Gladstone government recognised the need to legislate and provide for the protection of public health. In the Local Government Board Act of 1871, the Poor Law Board was replaced by the Local Government Board. In 1872 the structure of local government was further developed establishing Sanitary Authorities to deal with drainage, sewage and the outbreaks of infectious diseases. The Urban Sanitary Authorities were elected but the Rural Sanitary Authorities used the same personnel as the Union, consequently there was little difference from the Poor Law Unions. Tolworth was in the area supervised by the Kingston Rural Sanitary Authority.

During the 1880s the effectiveness of current means of provision for the protection of public health can be seen

William Ewart Gladstone, Prime Minister for four periods between 1868 and 1894

and evaluated by what happened in Tolworth. In the Surrey Comet of 18 June 1881, it was reported that the Kingston Rural Sanitary Authority was discussing the provision of a hospital to isolate people who had serious infections like tuberculosis, and who were not paupers. Suggestions were made for a hospital in an isolated area.

By early 1884 it seems that discussion had progressed and there was a proposal to build a hospital in Red Lion Road. Locally there was opposition on the grounds that this was a damp, low-lying clay area and that a more suitable place could be found. Moreover, it was maintained that the Red Lion Road was "teeming with children" who would be vulnerable to the germs. The major landowners: Mr. Eghill, Lord Egmont, and Lord Lovelace, supported the opposition and said they would claim compensation because such a hospital would reduce the value of their holdings. Mr Dowson, a land surveyor, said that water lay 2 feet deep in adjoining plots.

An original door in Tolworth Hospital

In May 1886, it was agreed that the Infectious Diseases Hospital would be built in Red Lion Road by the Kingston Rural Sanitary Authority. A loan was made by the Local Government Board, and in 1889 the isolation hospital was opened.

DIPHTHERIA AND THE SURBITON
SEWERS

TO THE EDITOR

Sir - Your remark in your last issue, "The preva-
lence of diphtheria in Surbiton leads one to ask
whether the sewers are properly ventilated," gives me
the opportunity of expressing my opinion on this subject, which is worthy of investigation, affecting as it
does the lives and well-being of the residents in the
neighbourhood.

Drainage is a question which is not sufficiently un-
derstood, but it is one to which I have devoted much
attention, and made a matter of study; and as regards
the recent outbreak of diphtheria, I believe it has
arisen entirely from the bad system of drainage,
though some few have attributed the infection to
milk.

Many of the cases occurred long before there was
any illness in Mr Kerswell's family, and many long
after his dairy was closed. Many parties were
affected who received their milk from other dairies,
and it is worthy of note is that very few out of Mr
Kerswell's large number of customers were affected.

On the other hand, in every case that I have attended I have found the bad system of drainage to be
the cause of the disease. I have invariably pointed
out the defects to the parties concerned and those who
have been able to carry out my suggestions have since
been free from all such complaints.

It is scarcely credible, that in the thickly populated
districts of Surbiton there are only three ventilators in
the sewer, and two of these in an almost uninhabited
part; whilst in most of the houses and cottages, the
pipes from the sculleries, sinks, and baths and the
overflow pipes of the cisterns are in direct communication with the main drains and sewers; consequently
the bad gases are forced back through these several
channels into the dwelling houses, poisoning the
inmates, and the weak and delicate fall victims.

Until something is done to remedy the present system, we can only expect recurrences of this or similar
maladies, and consequent victims, especially at those
seasons of the year when the winds and floods com-
bine to obstruct the free outflow of the sewage and
gases into the Thames.

I am, Sir, your obedient servant,
R. COLLUM, M.D.

December 2, 1880

The Surrey Comet, 4th December, 1880
page 4, column 6

The issue of drainage

The discussions concerned with the building of the hospital highlighted the chief problem for Tolworth development, namely the desperate need for an adequate drainage system. This was also the responsibility of the Rural District Sanitary Authority. As early as 1879 we learn from the Surrey Comet that Mr Justice Straight, who owned Woodside in Tolworth, had written to the Surbiton Improvement Commissioners asking them to extend their system to his property. He was, of course, aware of the 9 acres nearby which would be usable for building. This request was refused.

The Rural Sanitary Authority had a responsibility for a large area around Kingston, including Esher and the Dittons but not Kingston itself, and in the 1880s it had provided for those areas a drainage and sewage system at a reasonable cost to ratepayers. Tolworth and Hook were areas of more scattered population, and so were outside the scheme. In the letters column of the Surrey Comet in December 1880, a letter had appeared from a doctor, reporting on the recent outbreak of diphtheria due to bad sewers.

The correspondence blossomed and occupied the columns of the Comet for months, until the Editor put a stop to it in the 2nd April edition of 1881, regretting that the correspondence had become "personally disputatious". The heated dispute was actually over questions of civil engineering and the ventilation of sewers, with Messrs. Forde, Crimp and Cooper jumping on the bandwagon launched by Dr. Collum and resisted, futilely in the end, by Rowley W.C. Richardson, Chairman of the Surbiton Improvement Commissioners (and author of the history of this phase of Surbiton's growth). Clearly, this was a hot issue - action was needed if Tolworth was to develop.

In August 1888 the Surrey Comet reported a meeting of ratepayers, including residents of Red Lion Road, demanding that the Rural Sanitary Authority come up with a drainage scheme for Tolworth like the schemes for Esher and Long Ditton. The chairman was the Rev R.E. Johnson, the curate at St Matthew's.

The Sanitary Authority proposed a scheme which would have cost 3/- in the pound of the rateable value of the houses – far too expensive for the people of the area. Kavanagh, a builder and a leading light in the Tolworth community, proposed that while a scheme like that proposed was needed, this figure was too high for the district. This proposal was dropped in February 1889. It is interesting to note that some of the people of Tolworth were already by this time discussing the prospect of joining up with Surbiton.

In the spring of 1889 a new, less expensive, scheme was proposed. When the Rural Sanitary Authority refused to alter its course, the local committee, led by Mr Kavanagh and the Rev R.E. Johnson, took the matter to the Local Government Board in Whitehall, which set up a public enquiry. More acrimonious letters appeared in the Surrey Comet between the Sanitary Authority and the local committee. Eventually the Rev. Johnson produced a letter written to himself from the Local Government Board saying that it would not give a loan for the Rural Sanitary Authority's proposals as they were too expensive.

In 1891 a new scheme was proposed, a loan was made and pipes for drainage were being laid by 1892, and a sewage farm was developed. These events may seem mundane, but they illustrate the urgent need for honest, democratic and efficient local government if sound urban development was to take place.

The long-term problems of local government, however, could only be solved by new legislation, as was appreciated by some contemporaries. The Surbiton Review for example, in reporting the issue, remarked on the need for genuinely democratic government in rural areas. In 1894 the Local Government Act established Rural

The offices of Surbiton Urban District Council

District Councils in place of the Sanitary Authorities, and Urban District Councils in place of Improvement Commissioners. Both were elected by ratepayers (who were virtually all men over 21). For a short time, Tolworth was administered by Kingston Rural District Council, but in 1895 Tolworth, with Hook and Chessington, was taken into Surbiton Urban District Council. Although this may seem an arcane matter, it was a significant one for Tolworth. Until this date, Tolworth was a settlement outside the main urban development of the area. However, from this time onwards, it is seen and established as part of a significant London suburb.

Tolworth into the 20th century

Surbiton Council welcomed the new addition of land and councillors, and ordered a report on the facilities. In reporting on the sewage farm, a speaker remarked that there was not much to say and what there was would not be agreeable! Attention was paid

Houses in Douglas Road

to the state of the roads, and street lighting was provided from the Fishponds for another half mile into Tolworth. The 1890s and the early years of the 20th century saw a huge increase in house building with firms like Parkers, Cook's, Adam's and Ransome's buying up building plots as soon as they were available. In this way Douglas Road, Worthington Road and parts of Ellerton Road were filled with suitable family houses.

The change to a more urban outlook, however, was gradual. At the turn of the century, a rabbit could be bought for sixpence (2½p) outside the Red Lion, and water-cress at a farthing a bunch. Mr Stamford was the blacksmith who took care of the horses, while his brother, known as an engineer, could mend bicycles or steamrollers. There was no garage as yet, and the road that is now the A307 was only a track frequented by gypsies and by farmers driving animals to Guildford market.

As the twentieth century opened, Tolworth retained its rural character. The following incident illustrates this. One of the most determined developers, Stephen Kavanagh, wanted to develop land along the Ewell Road, between the church and Tolworth. On the corner of Egmont Road there was a pond which had been provided for horses. Kavanagh bought the plot, cleared the pond and replaced it with a drinking fountain. On July 29, 1901, the fountain was formally opened with great ceremony. Some 500 children processed to the music of the Surbiton Brass Band. In the afternoon the children were treated to a hearty tea at Tolworth Lodge Farm. Later they returned to the fountain, each with a large bun, where a further ceremony took place in the evening.

Tolworth at the beginning of the century was a busy place. The most important employment was the brick works. In 1903 the brickyard in Red Lion Road had been bought by Mr Pigott and was later run by his son, trading under the name of the Tolworth Brick Company. Another source of employment was the Royal Windsor Laundry in Lenelby Road, in the hands of a Mr Groves of Windsor who had bought it. The laundry, using the services of 80 to 100 local girls, served the large houses on the hill until the 1920s. With the use of vans after the war, the laundry provided a service for customers as far away as Oxshott and Weybridge.

As the population was growing and becoming more involved in Surbiton, two further amenities were provided. In August 1903 the electric light station opened, which offered to homes and shops "a clean, brilliant and healthy light". In 1900 the first horse-bus travelled from the Red Lion to Kingston. This was replaced by a tram in 1906, which linked Tolworth to Surbiton and Kingston.

Under the Education Act of 1902, Education Committees of County Councils were made responsible for the provision of appropriate schools in their own areas. In Tolworth, St. Matthew's School remained as a Church School, but as it was overcrowded, the Surrey County Education Committee needed to find land to build another elementary school. It was not until 1910 that this problem was solved, with the building of a school between Douglas Road and Red Lion Road (which is still with us: Tolworth Junior School) - see page 79.

The Church Hall today - the cornerHOUSE theatre

Under a new incumbent, the Rev. Jonathan Seaver, St Matthew's took on a new lease of life. To keep in contact with families, District Visitors were appointed, who sold the Parish Magazine, collected money for the Provident Fund and for the sick club subscriptions. In recognition of the inadequacy of the church building to provide for the social and spiritual needs of the new families, the church bought a site on the corner of Douglas and Ravenscar roads and built a parish hall which was opened in 1908. This would be an important social centre throughout the century.

By the outbreak of the First World War, therefore, it would be fair to say that Tolworth north of the Red Lion Road, was developed as an urban area, with family houses on roads either side of the Ewell Road. The census return in 1901 had been 2458, but in 1911 it was 4932.

South of the Red Lion Road there were still three working farms, and large tracts of common land remained. This was inviting development, which would take place ten years later. Francis Clayton, one of the founding churchwardens of St. Matthew's, died in 1912 - the end of an era. He would have been amazed at what followed.

CHAPTER 6

THE INTER-WAR YEARS

In 1918 it was claimed that the war to end wars had been fought and won. Sadly, we know that this was not true. But what had ended was the ordered pattern of assumptions and expectations of life in Edwardian Britain. On the European stage, the Habsburgs' rule in Austria[67], which had lasted for centuries, had gone. In Russia the Romanovs had been swept away by revolution in 1917[68] and the map of central Europe had been redrawn. In Britain, women for the first time were given the vote in General Elections and the Labour Party was no longer just a party of protest but was poised to replace the divided Liberal Party as the leading opposition voice. In just over

five years Labour's leader, Ramsay Macdonald, would be the first Labour Prime Minister. In Tolworth, these major political changes would have their repercussions over the next two decades.

The declaration of peace in November 1918 marked the beginning of a busy winter for every town and

65

War Memorial, Ewell Road, unveiling, July 1920

village in Britain. Boat loads of troops were returning from France to be demobilised and to take up life again as civilians. Although each man had his rations and pay for a month, there was an urgent need to place men in work. Local tribunals were set up to find employment. Money was collected for the Red Cross to help nurse the disabled. By 1922 the British Legion was founded to provide a meeting place for ex-servicemen, to provide for leisure activities, and to represent their interests. A branch was opened in Hollyfield Road for the ex-servicemen of Tolworth and Surbiton.

The problems of post-war reorganisation were further complicated by the Spanish flu[69], which was sweeping through Britain. In 1919 the Tolworth Isolation Hospital was full to capacity and many deaths were recorded in the area.

The first significant event after the Armistice[70] was the General Election. Lloyd George called it late in 1918 because he wanted a mandate at the Peace Conference which was to be held in 1919, in Paris. This was known as the "Khaki Election". It was memorable as the first General Election giving women the vote. The electorate gave the coalition of Conservatives and some Liberals 530 MPs, the Labour Party 60 MPs, and the Independent Liberals 29. Tolworth was part of the Kingston constituency for which the results were:

T.H.D. Campbell – Conservative Coalition: 13,395
T.H. Dumper – Labour: 2,502
A.E. Ely – Liberal Coalition: 2,352

Mr Dumper was personally well-known in Tolworth as the landlord of the Red Lion Public House. He was a Justice of the Peace and the Parish Poor Law Overseer. Since the turn of the century he had served on the Surbiton Urban District Council and had been instrumental in the purchase of the land for the Alexandra Recreation Ground and the allotments by the Council. In this he was supported by a nucleus of Labour supporters. In 1934 Tolworth returned another Labour Councillor in the person of Mr H.G. Reynolds, JP. He was later elected as an Alderman. In 1950 his son, Mr D. Reynolds, was also elected as a Labour Councillor for Tolworth West and served as the representative of that ward until 1978. He was elected by the Kingston Council as Mayor in 1974.

During the years following the war the dislocation of demobilisation and the sudden change in demand to meet domestic rather than military needs caused disturbance among working people throughout Britain. Men who had suffered in the trenches and women who had enjoyed wider opportunities in work were not prepared to return to the subservience and poverty of the pre-war days. Trades Union were, in many places and in different occupations, expressing the disaffection of these workers. In Tolworth this was evident in two different groups. In March 1919 a meeting was held concerning the working conditions of domestic servants. It was agreed, amongst other matters, that the servants should have two weeks paid holiday away from the employing family annually. A similar attitude among building workers is seen in a letter to the Surrey Comet in May 1919 from a Mr Lloyd of Pyne Road, reporting that local employers were advertising work at only 1/3d, 1/-, and 10d per hour, whereas the agreed Trade Union rates were 1/9d, 1/6d and 1/3d. The letter pointed out that the cost of living had risen by 113% since 1914.

In the post-war years, most people in Tolworth settled back into the life they had known before the war. Under a new incumbent Rev J.C. Banham (1918-28) St Matthew's

Rev J C Banham

Church continued to flourish. It had an electoral roll of 2007 – the highest in the diocese of Southwark. The yearly cycle of feasts and festivals continued as did the baptisms, weddings and funerals. In the community of Tolworth the church was not just a religious centre but a hub for a variety of social activities. The Church Hall in Douglas Road saw meetings of the Mothers' Union and the Young People's Union. The District Visitors continued on their rounds, collecting money for the Provident Society and selling the Parish Magazine. Perhaps the most significant in all this activity was the Scout Troop[71], which had been registered in 1909, and was very much encouraged by the vicar. Under his leadership the Scouts became a force in Tolworth, enhancing the lives of many young people. Not only did they win local proficiency competitions but also they had a football team, a cricket club and a bugle band.

On 26 February 1931, the Surrey Comet graphically illustrated the great changes taking place. The article reviews the building of houses (1,800 in the 3 years immediately prior). The Editor remembers that although Tolworth Lodge Farm was still at that time being run by the Hipwell family, the land had already been sold for development.

The Kingston bypass, 1927

It must be remembered that until the building of the by-pass, Tolworth was somewhat isolated. The ancient road from Kingston to Ewell joining up with Stane Street (A29) was still the main road to the South Coast but other roads (including what is now the A307 through Esher and Ripley) were little more than bridle tracks or drove ways. The coming of private cars, commercial vans and lorries and public buses and coaches demanded the development of a road system for Britain. A series of meetings known as the London Arterial Road Conference was held in the period 1912-16 to decide where the arterial roads should be built. Consequently the route of the Kingston by-pass was decided.

This was built in the early 1920s and opened on 27 October 1927. It was a significant development for the whole of Surrey because it linked London and Portsmouth on a fast road not going through Kingston. In fact, the full original intention of this new road was frustrated as soon as the road was finished: houses, and factories like Plessey and the Gala

Kingston by-pass at Hook

70

cosmetics factory, were built on either side of the new road with slip roads and junctions. This excessive number of hazards not only slowed down the traffic but also contributed to accidents. In 1997 the Kingston Council imposed a speed limit of 50 miles an hour on this road, which had been intended to be a fast through road.

In 1935 the Restriction of Ribbon Development Act was passed through Parliament to prevent further development of the kind that had been experienced along the Kingston by-pass.

Major house building

The world war left behind many problems for the coalition Government and Lloyd George, and housing was one of the major issues. No house building had been undertaken since 1916; building materials were in short supply and the national economy was weak. Although there had been a serious reduction in the number of able working men through loss of life in the war, unemployment was a serious problem. Builders' wages, especially for

71
David Lloyd George in about 1920

skilled men, were at an all-time high, averaging £5-0-7d a week in 1918 as against £2-10-0d in 1914. The Government, recognising the need for more houses, encouraged local Councils to make provision for low-cost rented accommodation, by enacting the Town Planning Act of 1919, which offered a subsidy to Councils. This national move had echoes in Tolworth. As early as June 1919, the Surrey Comet reported a discussion on the need to build, and mentioned the Tolworth nurseries at the end of the Red Lion Road. In July 1919 the Surbiton Urban District Council decided to build 50 houses on the site of Fullers Farm and the nurseries.

However, it was not Council housing which would dominate Tolworth but houses built privately for owner occupation with financial assistance from the Government. From 1920 to about 1935 the land which had been farm land or common land was covered with new roads, houses and garden fences. The last farms to remain were Tolworth Court Farm, which was being run until the end of the 20th century, and Tolworth Lodge Farm. It was not until 1931 that the Hipwell family gave up farming and this land was sold to developers.

1920s built housing in Cotterill Road

The financial arrangements for the conversion of farm land into private housing estates were well organised. A developer would purchase a sizeable area of land from the owners (some of whom were members of the same families who had acquired the land at the time of enclosures). The developer would be responsible for laying out the roads, for providing drainage and sewage and would then sell land on to individual builders in plots. There were several builders at work in Tolworth including Wimpey's (Elmbridge Avenue) and Thoroughgoods, a local firm which had been building in Surbiton at the turn of the century. Thoroughgoods were working in the Hamilton Avenue area. There was also Cronk, who specialised in blocks of four terraced houses.

I'm glad we bought our house through the Halifax Building Society — they gave us splendid terms.

Large funds are available for Home-buying. Last year this famous Society advanced over £21,000,000 for Property-purchase.

ASK FOR THE LATEST BOOKLET

LOCAL AGENT

EDGAR STURMAN, 18, Long Causeway, PETERBOROUGH

The price of houses was subsidised by the Government at £160 per house. It had long been recognised that there was a strong demand for more housing around London and other cities. In a time of world-wide depression, Government sponsored building was seen not only as a way to make more houses, but also as a way to reduce unemployment and stimulate the economy.

By the late 1920s labour costs had dropped, Building Societies[72] were lending at a lower rate and only demanding a 10% deposit. Prices of semi-detached houses varied from about £600-£850 with size; terraced houses were often cheaper.

Most of the houses were of essentially the same design, with two reception rooms and a kitchen on the ground floor, and two bedrooms and a small room with toilet and bathroom and airing cupboard on the first floor. Since the great impetus for building had been the coming of the Kingston bypass, the provision of garage space was considered important. Actually, at the time, very few of the early occupants could afford both a mortgage and a car, so the garages were used as storage to keep tools etc. for the good-sized gardens. After 1945 small cars, like Austin 7s, were gradually replaced by larger cars which did not fit into the garages! The roads were not wide enough to meet the needs of the developing size and design of traffic and the wide verges of grass, often with trees, which had been included in the development made the issue of parking a permanent problem. While a family with 2 to 3 children fitted the three-bedroom semi-

A pair of houses with garages, on Hook Rise North, by-pass service road

74

detached, the fact that there was so little variety also created problems. There were very few flats built, suitable for single people, or larger houses for families of more than two generations. There was practically no social housing or property available tor let, or for older people requiring sheltered accommodation. One cannot but wish that more time and overall direction had been given to promote the planning of varied development.

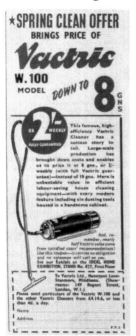

The inflow of so many people in such a short time (say 1930-35) must have overwhelmed the inhabitants. It offered many new opportunities and many challenges: the new houses needed furnishing, carpets and curtains. This must have contributed both to the prosperity of the new shops on the Broadway and also to the retail area of Kingston – especially Bentall's, which had been open in the centre of Kingston since 1867. No doubt the sales from these shops were promoted by the new system of hire purchase (a form of customer credit before the advent of credit cards). At the same time, domestic electrical goods like vacuum cleaners and fridges were coming onto the market and both enhanced the new houses and provided commercial opportunities.

New facilities for Tolworth

Most of the purchasers of the hundreds of new houses were families who had been living in the older suburbs. They tended to move out from locations nearer to the centre of London, on a radial. For example, many of the new people of Tolworth came from Clapham, Earlsfield or Wandsworth. They were urban people still working in London and requiring facilities for themselves and their families in a less crowded and more pleasant environment.

The most obvious need was for shops supplying basic goods. There was a parade of shops about a quarter of a mile towards Kingston from the Red Lion, but even with delivery this would have been inconvenient. Consequently the Ewell road was replaced in 1931 between Tolworth Lodge Farm and the site of Tolworth Court Farm with a straight road. This was the basis of the Tolworth Broadway which was opened in 1936. 57 shops were built,

Tolworth Broadway later, around 1958

each with a three-bedroom flat above. The freehold of such a shop and flat could be bought for £1,850. The Broadway boasted a wide variety of traders, including men's and women's outfitters, shoe shops and jewellers, and it included one of the first Tesco Stores. Although the shops were developed for people living in the local roads, they were often a long walk from customers' houses. Delivery boys on bicycles were a common sight.

The opening of the Kingston by-pass had been the event which had stimulated the building of the semi-detached houses in Tolworth and the garages beside each one. Despite the expectations embodied in the new by-pass and all the new garages, public transport was still the usual method of travel. In 1906 a tram, running on rails, was introduced in Tolworth, running from the Red Lion to the gates of Richmond Park going through Kingston. In 1931 this was replaced by the trolley bus, Route 601, which was more able to react to other road users. 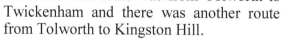 This route was from Tolworth to Twickenham and there was another route from Tolworth to Kingston Hill.

By 1959 London Transport had begun to replace the trolleybuses with double-decker Routemaster buses using diesel as a fuel. In 1962 the trolleybuses were withdrawn.

77

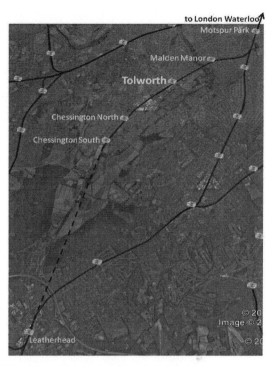

With the improved road system Tolworth became a hub for buses to Kingston and Kingston Hill, Epsom and Ewell, and Reigate and Guildford (although the routes to Guildford and Reigate have since been withdrawn). In 1938 a new railway line was opened. The plan was to link Wimbledon with Leatherhead, via Motspur Park, Worcester Park, Malden Manor, Tolworth and Chessington. Unfortunately the Second World War prevented the building of the line beyond Chessington.

Education

The huge growth in the population, particularly of families in the semi-detached houses, obviously meant that the school places provided locally were inadequate. By 1910 the Victorian Elementary School had been enlarged and a further school had been provided by the Surrey County Council. Until 1902 St. Matthew's School was a mixed school under a headmistress. In 1902 the headmistress was replaced by Edward Stokoe. He would play a very significant part in the development of education in Tolworth. By 1903 he had set up a system of rewards for attendance and progress. A wider curriculum was introduced to include domestic science for the girls and football and cricket for the boys. Science lessons were introduced with practical work and children were taken to the swimming baths in Kingston.

However the school buildings on Ewell Road were inadequate.

With the 1902 Education Act, it became the duty of the County Councils, through their Education Committees, to make provision for the schooling needs af their residents. Voluntary Schools (like Church Schools) continued under their existing managers, but the Council was required to make other provision as required.

In 1902, Edward Stokoe was appointed as Headmaster to St. Matthew's School. Mr. Stokoe endorsed the view of the Schools Inspector that there was a serious problem of overcrowding. Consequently, the County Council in 1905 provided temporary accommodation for Mr. Stokoe and his boy pupils. St Matthew's remained a voluntary-aided Church school for infants and girls, with its own identity.

Subsequently, the County Council acquired the site between Douglas Road and Red Lion Road where it firstly set up temporary accommodation for the boys. Later, in 1910, permanent accommodation was built on this site, for boys and infants. The girls

Tolworth Primary School, Douglas Road

remained in the original school buildings until 1974, when St. Matthew's School was rebuilt on Langley Avenue (on the very edge of the parish) - still as a voluntary-aided Church school. At this point, both of the schools became Primary Schools, both catering for boys and girls aged 5-11 - one a Church school and the other under the Kingston Education Committee.

Both schools are still open at the time of writing this book: St. Matthew's School, Langley Road; and Tolworth Primary School, Douglas Road.

Churches

Although it is certainly true to say that after the First World War churches had lost the dominance they had enjoyed in Victorian times, nonetheless the Church was still an important source of social cohesion in the life of the communities served. With the influx of so many people, the main denominations sought to provide for the population.

Our Lady Immaculate, RC

The Roman Catholics, whose church was St Raphael's in Surbiton, appointed a lively priest to oversee the new Roman Catholic parish of Tolworth in the person of Father Redding. The original suggestion was that there should be a new church building in Thornhill Road named for an English saint. Father Redding did not compromise. He wanted a sizeable site on the main Ewell road and, fortunately for the Roman Catholics, he won. Our Lady Immaculate (or Olie as it is affectionately known by local people) stands on the main road on a prominent corner, on land bought by the Roman Catholic diocese of Southwark. A simple hall was created which was used for Mass on High Days and Sundays. In 1936 a chapel was built on the site of the presbytery – its cost was an amazingly low figure of £100 due to the industry of men using their own skills and time. This was a beginning: after the Second World War, Our Lady Immaculate would emerge as the fine building gracing Tolworth Broadway that it is now.

St George's, Church of England

The houses which were built to the west of Ewell Road, for instance in Princes Avenue and Hamilton Avenue, lay in the parish of St Matthew's. By 1929 the Parish Church Council accepted that it would be necessary to provide for the new residents. The

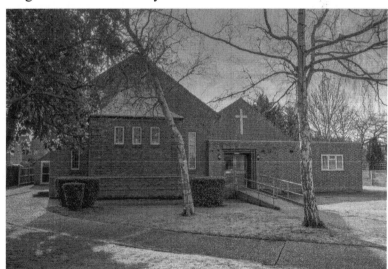

Council resolved to buy a plot of land in the area where the domestic houses were being erected.

Consequently a large plot in Hamilton Avenue was obtained. A group of PCC members oversaw the work and were known as the St Matthew's Church Extension Committee – a telling name which suggests that St George's was seen as an enterprise dependent on St Matthew's. An appeal was launched in February 1930 with a target of £3000 and in the first six months £800 was raised. The new residents gave generously and by 1933 250 of them were making regular donations. The "25 Churches Fund" which had been set up by the Diocese provided £1000, and an anonymous donation provided £500.

A further loan of £1000 made the building of the church possible. The first building was a simple one used for both Sunday worship and social activities. It was consecrated in June 1934. The relatively simple first Church building was set in a large plot of land, which had been purchased because it would later enable a larger and more complex centre to be erected. The first Minister at St George's was the Rev E.H. Atkey.

Congregational/URC Church

There was a strong, well established Methodist Church on the Ewell Road and a Baptist church in Langley Avenue, so it was appropriate that the new Free Church should be a Congregational one (which became a United Reformed Church in 1972). A plot of land on the corner of Elgar Avenue and Raeburn Avenue was acquired and the new church was completed in 1934. The building, which had a simple dignity, soon became a new centre of social life.

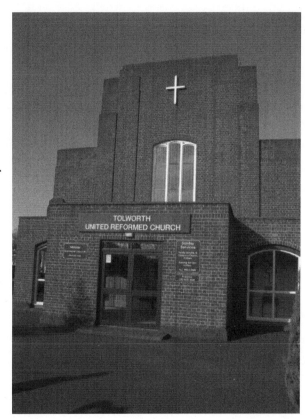

Leisure activities

The new residents had much to be grateful for to Mr Dumper who, soon after the war, had persuaded the Surbiton Urban District Council to purchase a large piece of land between Alexandra Drive and Elgar Avenue as a public recreation ground. It fulfilled the functions of park, sports field for football and cricket, tennis courts, children's playground and allotments. In addition an open-air swimming pool was laid out in 1934 on the other side of Raeburn Avenue. These provided welcome and secure spaces in what could have been an overpopulated area.

At the same time, commercial enterprises were opening to provide for other leisure needs of the new community. A new public house, the Toby Jug, opened near the railway station. Perhaps the most exciting of all was the new cinema which opened on the corner of the bypass and the Broadway.

In 1933 Oscar Deutsch opened his first London cinema in Kingston; it was followed the next year by the Odeon in Tolworth which opened on 9th June 1934 with Eddie Cantor in "The Kid From Spain". In a world without television in every home it is not difficult to understand the importance of moving, and then speaking pictures. The cinema provided a good, peaceful, meeting place for adults, especially courting couples, and a new insight into the world beyond one's own immediate experience. On any Saturday morning, children, each clutching his or her precious sixpence, would queue to see the special children's cartoons. The cinema organ would strike up and the children would sing, as loud as possible:

Every Saturday morning,

Where do we go?

Getting into mischief?

Oh dear, no!

To the Mickey Mouse Club,

With our badges on,

Every Saturday morning,

At the O-de-on!

Life in Tolworth in the 1930s must have been exciting. So many new people to meet, so many new things to do. So many new opportunities for both adults and children. Such a contrast to the continuity of earlier decades. Surely for a few years Tolworth must have been a place of hope.

But, as we all know, it was not to last. The men who built the houses packed up their tools and returned to the factories - the Depression was over. Unemployment was down, but war was on the way again. There would not be Peace In Our Time.

CHAPTER 7

TOLWORTH POST WAR

War and its immediate aftermath

The summer of 1939 brought Tolworth, as everywhere else in Britain, daily nearer to the inevitable conflict with Germany. No one could doubt, as they heard of the events in Europe that soon the war would be declared – as it was on the fateful Sunday, 3 September 1939. Already by that time preparations had been made. Ration books had been printed, transport for troops organised, gas masks produced and plans for the evacuation of millions of children from areas vulnerable to bombing had been achieved by the Government. Locally, in Tolworth, people were preparing by blacking out their windows and organising their own air raid shelters. Some were joining local branches of the ARP (Air Raid Precautions wardens), the Royal Voluntary Service Corps or the Home Guard. ("Dad's Army" may seem

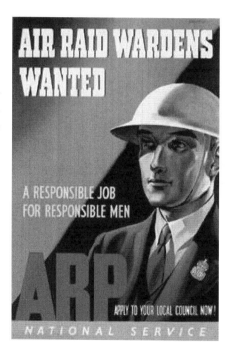

entertainment 70 years on, but in 1939 it was grim reality – the ability of people to work together in their locality was vital for success against the terrifying, and real, threat of invasion.)

The most dramatic immediate reaction to the declaration of war in Britain was the organisation of the evacuation of children. In the early days of the war, Tolworth was involved in this. In fact as the weeks passed and Britain found herself in the phoney war[73] period, the children returned home. For the most part, Tolworth's children remained at home, but Tolworth was not an area to receive evacuees either. This was probably sensible.

Although near to London there was only one German bombing raid that was aimed at a Tolworth target. It was on 2 September 1940 when the targets were the Nash and Thompson arms works in Oak Croft Road, and Siebe Gorman, where diving equipment was manufactured, on the by-pass. Otherwise, the effect of the bombing was random and

Gun turret made by Nash & Thompson for the Lancaster bomber

90

sporadic, although individual houses were destroyed and other property was damaged by blast. 27 people from Tolworth were killed in the raids. Perhaps more disturbing for the inhabitants were the flying bombs later in the war - in the summer of 1944. Without any warning these pilotless weapons would fall from the sky bringing death and destruction. On 17 June 1944, a single doodlebug fell in Tolworth Park Road killing 12 people and destroying five houses. But compared with many parts of London Tolworth remained more or less intact.

Nevertheless there was a great deal to do by way of rebuilding and restoring once the war was over, with money from the War Damage funds. It was not until the Festival of Britain[74], six years after the war had ended, in 1951, that people could feel that with many worn and broken everyday things renewed they could look forward to the future. Not just material things, but the social fabric of life, with soldiers demobilised and home. Perhaps one of the most fruitful aspects of the years immediately after the war was the growth in local clubs and societies supporting social life.

In Tolworth these included the Tolworth and District Leisure Gardeners Society in the Alexandra Park and the Surbiton Historical Society. The Berrylands Lawn

Berrylands Lawn Tennis Club house

The Youth Fellowship relaxing

Tennis Club was revived (with the lower grass courts restored - they had been dug up for allotments during the war[75]) and the Parish Players (linked to St Matthew's) took to the stage in the Douglas Road Parish Hall. Young people were well supported in the Scouts and Guides, Cubs and Brownies. The churches played an important part. St Matthew's and St George's weekly Guild meetings offered a varied programme of film shows, concerts and talks to its 300 members. For teenagers, the youth club met on Saturday evenings and twice during the week, with 60 members. This kind of activity was not exclusively a Tolworth phenomenon, but here, as elsewhere in Britain, it was one of the most important extensions into the peacetime world of the sense of community which had grown so much in the preceding decade of conflict and fear.

Church life – post war

A further example of the growing self assertion of the people of Tolworth can be seen in the development of the churches and church community in the post-war

period. The first Catholic church building had been erected in the 1930s to support both religious and secular activities. There was a large patch of available land around the Catholic chapel and later in the 1930s the diocese bought the adjoining houses - numbers 401 and 403 Ewell Road. This made it possible to build a new church - one that would be fitting for Catholic services in this growing, self-confident congregation. In 1953, Father Redding assured the congregation that steps were being taken to achieve this, despite the fact that materials were in short supply. In 1958 the church of Our Lady Immaculate was completed and it was consecrated in May 1963. The cost was £60,000, £42,000 of which had been given by the congregation over 22 years. In the period after the war the Catholic inhabitants of Tolworth articulated the urgent need for a Catholic primary school under the auspices of the church in Tolworth. Father Redding supported this aspiration, and went to great trouble to persuade the Diocese and the County Council that this project should be undertaken on grounds of religious freedom and social justice. Eventually, in December 1950, permission to build was given and on 1 September 1953 the school was opened.

The story at St George's (Church of England) was somewhat similar. Like the Catholics, the congregation of St George's felt that their building, although well constructed, was not adequate for both religious services and social events. The congregation would have favoured building a new church and retaining the original building for social purposes. The Mission Hall in Pyne Road had been sold in the 1930s to raise money to build

St. George's Church, raising £515. A further £600 had been raised from the insurance company. At the general meeting in February 1951, the Vicar pointed out that the project favoured by the congregation would have a cost of £50,000 and was going to be out of the question. Consequently, it was deemed impossible to build a new permanent church building, but a hall was proposed instead, at £6000. This was a poor judgement. The cheaply built hall was not really suitable for the needs of church life. Moreover it was placed on land which would be required for sale 15 years later to meet further parish debts.

The Victorian church of St Matthew's, built in 1875, stood as William Matthew Coulthurst had left it. It was, 100 years later, still a beautiful and much loved example of 19th-century Gothic church architecture, but it lacked adequate heating, committee rooms, and what social space was provided was unsuitable for the life of the contemporary church. Moreover, the Parish Hall was in Douglas Road – the best part of half a mile away.

Fortunately, in 1972, when a member of the congregation, Miss Sitzler died, she left the bulk of her estate to St. Matthew's Church, and stipulated that the money could only be used for church fabric or building. Architects were employed to convert the church building and make it more suitable for congregational use. Parts of the aisles were walled off to make a Chapel and a room suitable for teaching, and room at the west end with a kitchen was provided for meetings and social events. This was named the Sitzler Room in honour of the generous donation.

During the succeeding decade the Parish Hall in Douglas Road, being by then needed less for immediate church use, was leased to the Douglas Centre Trust, specially created to support community activities. The building has since further enhanced its life as the cornerHOUSE community theatre.

Entertainment

We have noted that role that local societies played in the emerging leisure culture of Tolworth after the war, and we have noted the role of the local churches. These two forces combined in the development of what has become a really active, serious community theatre in Tolworth - the cornerHOUSE. The St. Matthew's and St. George's congregations, and especially their Youth Fellowship, from the 1940s through the 1960s started by putting the Parish Hall in Douglas Road into excellent use as a theatre. By the 21st century the cornerHOUSE was staging ambitious theatre, new writing, single act plays and was also home to a film club – the cinema comes back to Tolworth 50 years after the demolition of the Odeon.

Rock music was also supported on an impressive scale in Tolworth in the 1960s. The Toby Jug pub was "accustomed to presenting cabaret acts for its suburban clientele"[76] but, almost despite itself[77], provided a home for rock bands through the decade, and officially opened as a music venue in March 1968. The array of

96

famous bands that played there is extraordinary, including Led Zeppelin, The Yardbirds, Fleetwood Mac, Jethro Tull. Joe Cocker, John Mayall's Bluesbreakers and David Bowie for the first night of his Ziggy Stardust tour in 1972. This rock scene moved to a pub in Tooting, and the Toby Jug was demolished in the early years of the 21st century.

The corner of Tolworth roundabout remains a mecca for leisure - there is now the Charrington Bowl, one of the biggest facilities for ten-pin bowling in Europe. On another corner, a further entertainment "hub" for Tolworth, the Odeon Cinema had stood, but was closed in 1959 and demolished in 1961, to make way for the Tolworth Tower. From the end of the 1960s until the opening of the cornerHOUSE film club in 2012, it required a visit to Kingston to go to the movies.

Another pub that became famous was just up the road at the next roundabout on the A3 – at Hook roundabout. The Ace of Spades road house was the centre of a different kind of entertainment, with its swimming pool and high diving board. There were "Roadhouse Nights" - drinks and cabaret - back in the 1930s (the 1932 Pathé newsreel of that title[78] is almost certainly filmed at the Ace of Spades), and in the 1950s Diana Dors and friends were desporting themselves in the road-house pool[79]. By the post-war decades, the Ace of Spades was declining. It burnt down in the mid 1950s. The same site is occupied in 2015 by a Wetherspoons pub, now called the Cap in Hand. In its hey-day, the Ace of Spades even built a private airstrip for its clientele, in the days when wealthy young people might dash about in their own aeroplanes.[80]

Diametrically across the Hook roundabout from the Ace of Spades, in Ace Parade, was a more modest establishment, the Tip-Top Café, patronised by another breed of worshippers of speed, with rather less disposable income. The by-pass was intended for those who used motors primarily to get somewhere fast, without getting snarled up in local streets, but others seized the opportunities offered. After the Second World War there grew up a class of young men (and a few women)[81] who could afford powerful motorcycles and were interested in speed, and the by-pass provided a proving ground for them. They gathered at the Tip-Top Café and became notorious as the boys who "did the ton" on this fine piece of roadway, and made bets about speed through the Tolworth underpass.

The Surbiton Croquet Club, in Alexandra Park, hosts the 2010 MacRobertson International Croquet Shield . (see note)

More sedate forms of entertainment were (and are still) provided for at the other end of Tolworth, in the big Alexandra recreation complex at the foot of King Charles Road[82]. Bowls, tennis, football, cricket, basketball and the home of one of the finest croquet clubs in England[83] are all hosted in these 25 acres, together with over 100 allotments. There is also a park – the Alexandra Millennium Green – created and maintained by the efforts of the local community when, in the 1980s, the Council of Kingston threatened to develop this area for housing,.

We have mentioned on page 104 the Tolworth Recreation Centre, another leisure facility for the people of Tolworth and the surrounding area, built as a shared resource with Tolworth Girls' School (formerly Tolworth Central School).

Anthony Trinkwon, neighbouring resident, mows the Alexandra Millennium Green (on a much-loved 1964 Massey-Ferguson 35X tractor)

Education

With the growth of population in the years immediately preceding the war, the raising of the school leaving age to 15 years, and the demand for a wider education to meet the needs of the modern economy, it was inevitable that there would be more and wider provision of education in Tolworth as elsewhere.

- By 1961 the secondary school in Fullers Way was clearly inadequate for boys as well as for girls, and the boys were moved to the new school near Hook roundabout, now known as Southborough High School.

- The Girls' School now occupied the whole of the Central School building, renamed as Tolworth Girls' School.

- There were school premises in Hollyfield Road which had originally been the Surbiton Central School. This had been renamed as Hollyfield School before it was moved to the site at the top of Surbiton Hill, which had previously been Surbiton Grammar School. It was this school that Eric Clapton attended, while going to art classes in the "Annex" in Ewell Road, next to the Fire Station.

- The former high school buildings in Hollyfield Road have been used since then by Kingston Council for adult education classes.

The hall, at LISC, converted and restored

- The little Victorian parish school on the Ewell Road which had been built by the first congregation of St Matthew's was also not serviceable for the needs of a primary school in the 20th century, and its buildings were replaced by a new open place school in Langley Road in 1974 – still St. Matthew's School. It should be noted that this was now on the edge of St Matthew's parish and strictly speaking outside Tolworth.

- That Victorian school building was occupied for nearly 20 years by the Metropolitan Police Force as Surbiton Police Station, and has since been returned to use as a school - for students from all over the world learning English and preparing for entrance to British universities. This transition happened in 2011 when the buildings were bought and comprehensively restored by the new school owners, who live near to Tolworth and operate as the London International Study Centre (LISC

- The development of the Sunray housing estate south of the by-pass had been interrupted by the advent of war. Consequently, a new primary school to serve the estate had not been constructed. In 1960 this omission was made good and the new school, Knollmead, was opened.

The first headmaster, Bill Bellerby, was a very lively, able man − highly respected, Mr. Bellerby cycled to school from his home in Guildford. It was a good start to the new school and an important contribution to life in Tolworth.

Local government

The most significant change of the post-war period was the major reorganisation of local government in London. In 1895, Tolworth had become part of the Surbiton Urban District, under the Surrey County Council. In 1936 Surbiton became a Borough; Tolworth was part of it.

In 1960, the Royal Commission on Local Government in Greater London (chairman Sir Edwin Herbert) published its results which led to the 1963 Act, under which a Greater London Council was created to perform strategic functions. Implemented in 1965, its powers included cross-borough development, overseeing transport, planning, sewage and other matters.

At first there was considerable opposition by the people of Tolworth to being drawn into the Greater London orbit in this way. The existing boroughs: Kingston, Malden & Coombe and Surbiton (including Tolworth) were merged to form the new Royal Borough of Kingston upon Thames. However, as the status of being part of a London Borough under the GLC became accepted, the additional facilities available both in Tolworth and in other parts of Kingston opened peoples' eyes to the advantages of the change.

An example of this is the Recreation Centre which was built next to the girls' school, at the end of Red Lion Road, and opened in November 1978. It was necessary to extend the Tolworth Girls School on account of increasing numbers. By pooling resources it became possible for the growing school community and for the people of Tolworth and the borough as a whole to acquire facilities which included a large hall for badminton, volleyball and other physical activities. This leisure centre now hosts one of the best gym clubs in Britain. A small hall was provided for squash. In addition a simple theatre with

A national karate competition in the Tolworth Leisure Centre (Saturday 4 August 2001)

a cafeteria made the Recreation Centre a popular meeting place for people in Tolworth and across the Borough of Kingston.

The amalgamation of the London boroughs, firstly under the Greater London Council, and then from 2000 the Greater London Authority, also had a significant effect on the life of Tolworth residents. A towering figure in London politics, Ken Livingstone, straddled both of those organisations, first as Leader of the GLC, then as elected Mayor for the GLA. His influence was felt locally most obviously in his regeneration of London's public transport. Tolworth is very well served by bus routes covering many local residential roads and linking Tolworth to Ewell, Epsom and New Malden nearby; to Putney Bridge and to Hounslow further off; as well as to Kingston and through Kingston to many destinations across London, and to Kingston Hospital.

Tolworth Hospital

The Fever Hospital in Red Lion Road, which had been built in 1889, saw a change of role after the war. Originally the purpose

105

of this hospital, sited away from housing, had been to isolate people with serious infectious diseases like cholera and diphtheria. An item in the Surrey Comet back in July 1905 had announced that an extension to the Isolation Hospital was opened with 12 cubicles for beds and a pavilion block of 30 further beds, making it a hospital of 110 beds. In 1906 a further extension was opened and in 1925, 1932 and 1935 further adjoining land was purchased, to a total of nine acres.

With the coming of the National Health Service[84] immediately after the war in 1948 the Isolation Hospital became part of the provision for the whole area and outside of the control of the local authority. In 1969 the hospital dropped the "Isolation" from its title - the modern development of antibiotics had created a world in which infection had lost its hold. Tolworth Hospital became a general hospital, used for patients of local doctors. A further 22 beds were added for geriatric patients.

The use of the hospital has undergone further radical change – it is now (in 2015) primarily a mental hospital serving the whole of South West London, but still with a number of vital beds for rehabilitation of local patients. The changes undergone by Tolworth Hospital have reflected the continuing changes in the structure of the National Health Service which itself continues to follow changes in medical practice.

Employment

Unlike Surbiton, Tolworth has never been primarily a commuter town. Originally, and indeed until the 1930s, it had been an agricultural area with its clay soil providing lush grass for dairy farmers. From 1871, bricks were produced from the clay in Fullers Farm at the far end of the Red Lion Road, as we know from census returns. This business was bought in 1903 by Mr Piggott and managed by his son. Later it traded under the title of the Tolworth Brick Company. In pre-war days, a whistle had sounded at 7 am for work to begin, and half an hour later one could hear steam being released. All this had stopped by 1932, when the clay pit was filled in and brickmaking ceased: it was on this site that Tolworth Central School, later Tolworth Girls School, was built.

Another source of local employment was the Windsor Steam Laundry in Lenelby Road.

This had originated in the later years of the 19th century and was bought by Mr. Groves in 1909. It was a flourishing business and with the use of vans for delivery took in work from as far afield as Wimbledon and Esher. Before the war, back in the 1920s this business employed 100 girls[85]. The closure of the laundry in the 1970s marked a loss of employment for female workers in the area. As in so many ways, machines (like the washing machine) had taken the place of human effort.

With the coming of the Kingston by-pass in 1927, new factories were built to take advantage of the efficient new transport system. There had been a major Government employment site along the southern edge of the by-pass from the Tolworth roundabout since before the war. Employment at this site

The Gala Cosmetics factory, Hook Rise

expanded during the war and in the 1950s it housed major offices of the Ministry of Defence, including the headquarters of surveying functions, and offices of the Ministry of Agriculture. Employment at the site was diminished to closure in the 1970s. The site - known as the Toby Jug site after the pub that had been at the corner - was bought by Tesco, the grocers, with a series of different promised uses that had still come to nothing in 2015 after many years of proposals. At the time of writing, Tesco's are planning a major housing development on the site.

Other major employers included Gala Cosmetics (the manufacturers of the Mary Quant range, and subsequently, through their proprietor Stanley Picker, sponsors of the arts in Kingston)[86], Siebe Gorman - diving equipment, and Decca opening in 1960 in Tolworth making records. In 1980 Decca's business suffered from competition and technical changes, and it was sold out to Racal in 1980. The Tolworth factory had been sold in 1965.

The Tolworth Tower was opened in 1963. One of the aims of this initiative was to provide more space for offices. This development caused more controversy than any other in the post-war period. The Tower occupied the site which had included the Odeon cinema which had closed in 1959. The development was designed by Richard Seifert, a well-known architect of the time, responsible also for the Centre Point tower in the heart of London's West End. Tolworth Tower reached nearly 265 feet in height – 22 stories – and was one of the tallest buildings in Britain at the time; it could be seen from miles around. The structure of glass and concrete was an innovation in suburban building. The ground floor was left to Fine Fair supermarket which provided Tolworth with another new employer – claiming to be the largest supermarket in the country.

On the higher stories, there was provision of a very large area of office space which was intended to be taken up by increasing local employment for the area. During the early years of the new Kingston Borough the Tower provided space for workers of Kingston Council, including the newly formed Education Department. The Home Office and the Driving Licence

Office also rented space. In 2005, a hotel (Travelodge) opened for business in the Tower (and is still, at the time of writing, operating with 120 rooms, and is also part of the operation of Tolworth Tower that the new owners and developers - see page 123 - intend to maintain in business). However, the 22 stories of the tower were never fully occupied. In the second decade of the 21st century, the original plans for office use were largely abandoned and a firm of developers very active in the Borough of Kingston, CNM, plan to convert many floors of the Tower to residential use and to rebuild the line of buildings that front the Broadway. This project is in its early phases at the time of writing this book, awaiting formal planning application.

The Broadway itself needed staff for the shops - over 80 in the Broadway itself, and nearly 140 including the run of Ewell Road. Immediately after the war, the range of shops had included two large Co-operative stores, Boots and Woolworths, two hardware shops, a ladies' dress shop and two gentlemen's outfitters, as well as newsagents, post office and banks. As the decades passed the pattern of shops changed. Many restaurants occupied premises that had previously supported privately owned retailers. New trades like nail bars, photo processors and computer repair shops appeared. The large supermarket Fine Fare gave way to a Marks & Spencer's food hall under Tolworth Tower and Radio Jackie opened in former Post Office premises on the opposite side of the Broadway, to provide information and entertainment for the people of Kingston Borough and the surrounding area.

The selection of trades available on the Broadway has changed at the end of the 20th century and in the first decades of the 21st. The restaurant and takeaway trade is dominant with 33 outlets in 2015, about 30% of the premises available in the whole strip. Moreover, these restaurants are providing cuisine from all over the globe, and there are groceries and delicatessen businesses also supplying food that would not have been seen in Tolworth 30 years ago – including Indian, Sri Lankan, Bulgarian, Thai, Polish, Pakistani, Chinese, Lithuanian. This is one consequence of the wide variety of people who have come to live in Tolworth since the Second World War. An informal review of the nationalities of those who manage shops in the Broadway in 2015 gives an interesting perspective on this diversity. It seems that about 35% of the shops in Tolworth are managed by people who have come from outside Britain. The largest group are from south-east Asia – 21%, including Indian and Sri Lankan. 7% come from East Asia and nearly 5% from the continent of Europe, mostly from Eastern Europe. Just under 4% come from the Middle East.

54-76 The Broadway in 2014

It seems to be the case in Tolworth that a substantial proportion of those settling here from abroad are qualified people pursuing careers in business, or in the professions such as law and medicine. Tolworth is being well served in its social and political life by these people coming in from outside – across the Borough we are fortunate that there are many residents coming from abroad who are willing to commit time to serve the borough politically and in community action. The congregation of Our Lady Immaculate, in particular, has not just assimilated many new people, particularly from Sri Lanka, but found in them new, active, facilitators of a healthy parish life. These people from all over the world have brought new ideas and energy to Tolworth, and in response Tolworth maintains a climate of successful integration.

Conclusion

Over a period of 140 years, Tolworth had ceased to be a hamlet within the parish of Long Ditton. It had become part of the sprawl of the suburb of Surbiton. The current Royal Borough of Kingston upon Thames, with a history, like Tolworth's, beginning in Saxon times, had enveloped Tolworth. Finally, in the 21st century, Tolworth is emerging as a place in its own right playing a full role in one of the world's most cosmopolitan cities – London.

THE STORY OF TOLWORTH

The borders of Tolworth Town in the 21st century - where should they be placed?

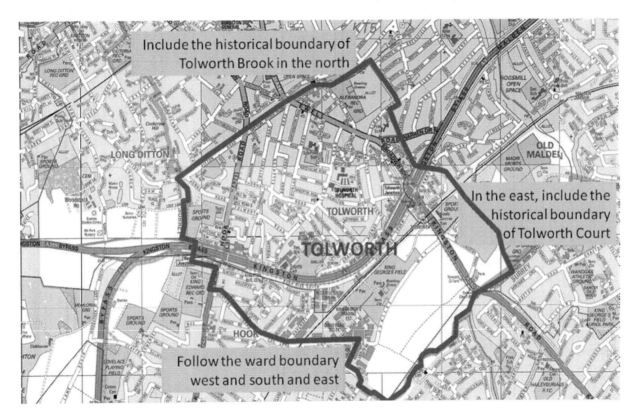

The answer is not straightforward: there are many competing sources that might be called upon in defining our borders - not just what the current Local Authority lays down. Clearly, a proper answer must have reference to our history. In Appendix B we make an attempt to answer the question of where our borders should be, and the diagram above gives our answer.

EPILOGUE

TOLWORTH RESURGENT?

We have seen through the course of this book that as the history of Tolworth has unfolded there have been several shifts in what one might call the "centre of gravity" of the town. For the longest part of its history, Tolworth existed as a self-contained hamlet, or just a manor and a few houses. We have seen that during the Middle Ages there were times when Tolworth had some "gravity" as a local administrative centre. At that time, Tolworth Manor stood for itself - a small centre of its own gravity.

Then, Tolworth began to gain significance because of its place on the map: on the road between the Royal Palaces of Hampton Court and Nonsuch; on the road from Hampton Court to the summer residence of the Archbishop of Canterbury, Croydon Palace. Tolworth retained and enhanced the "gravity" of local administrative importance, but the records indicate that the Manor began to find an identity in the wider world in relation to the "gravitational pull" of these stellar locations from which persons of importance travelled.

Then, much later, in the nineteenth century, the centre of gravity of Tolworth shifted radically: new development was coming from the north, and Tolworth's identity came to be defined in terms of its relationship with Surbiton. This "north biased" centre of gravity is what still characterises our town in its contemporary state, in the early decades of the 21st century.

But, is the centre of gravity shifting again? In this concluding section, we want to consider some of the characteristics of the town now, and try to identify any indications there are of the way that Tolworth might develop in the next 50 years.

The pull toward the north was given most of its initial impetus by the coming of the London and Southampton Railway in 1838. Enclosure came late to Tolworth and the railway age came early - these two huge influences wrenched it into a new orbit. Other "northward biased" developments, such as the building of the new Parish Church to the north of the town (1875) followed the line of pull of commercial development which followed the pull of the railway.

But, more recently, there have come some developments that may counteract this pull. There is another railway and another station −Tolworth Station, opened in 1938. This is on a minor branch line, to Chessington, but this railway was conceived as something a bit grander - a line to Leatherhead. The Second World War intervened a year after the new station opened, and it has not, so far, had much of a gravitational pull on the development of Tolworth. But it will.

The opening of one of the first almost motorway-grade by-passes in Britain, in 1927, added a gravitational pull to the south of the town, providing a new location for commercial development. However, the word "by-pass" tells it all: the effect of this gravitational disturbance was to create an orbit around Tolworth. However, because Tolworth, prior to this, had had such poor road connections, the new road did have the effect of putting Tolworth on the map. It had another effect - less desirable. The new road cut through the town with a barrier that subsequent generations have struggled to diminish. This was not all that obvious at the time the by-pass was built because it cut built-up Tolworth from the remnants of the common. But as soon as that land was developed - principally the Sunray estate - these new parts were most effectively cut off from the rest of Tolworth

There were some consequences of this later revolution in transportation that have, though, set up lesser gravitational disturbances that may, as time passes, draw the centre of gravity of the town away from the north. Colonel Seifert's Tolworth Tower was a development (1963) that was triggered by the heavy use of the by-pass and by location of the big roundabout at Tolworth. The by-pass was also, earlier, the catalyst for the development of a series of linked sites to accommodate Ministry of Defence establishment, in use from the 1930s and on beyond the War.

Neither of these developments made a great difference to the centre of gravity of Tolworth in their original development, other than by providing some new employment opportunities for Tolworth people. Indeed, both these developments were looking to a world outside Tolworth, opened up by the communication possibilities of the by-pass. Their location in Tolworth town was almost incidental: it was the road around Tolworth that was important in their conception.

But both of these developments have passed beyond their original purpose (and the MoD site has been closed for years and has been subject to monstrous planning wrangles). These sites are now emerging with the possibility of a new gravitational influence, and a new relationship with their home - Tolworth. For both sites, for different reasons, a re-purposing is almost certain: as housing.

When redeveloped, these two sites, between them, will add well over 1000 homes to the local housing stock, and all towards the south of the town. The plans unveiled for the Tower development at the time this book was being finalised include three new blocks next to the Tolworth Tower, 400 new homes and 60 serviced apartments in addition to retaining the hotel in the Tower (Kingston Guardian, 19/3/2015). With the

"Toby Jug" site now being planned entirely for housing, the projections there are for 700 houses (Surrey Comet, 19/9/2014), and there may be room for more with other developments under consideration for "roofing over" the underpass (see below). These will be different kinds of housing: there may be more child-less families and singles moving to the renovated Tolworth Tower site, and families to the old MoD site.

As these plans emerge, there is already a call, from the Council and others, for there to be investment in the infrastructure that will be required by the influx of new people into these houses. The first, and most urgent, call is for schools to be built - the new residents will swamp the schools in the town that are already overcrowded. But schooling is just the tip of the iceberg. For instance, Kingston Council has drawn attention to the fact that these new residents will need access to green spaces, and the Leader of the Council has already announced investment in such facilities, south of the A3 (Surrey Comet 12/09/2014), giving as context his expectation that "In the next five years, Tolworth is going to be an area of major redevelopment." Again, we are looking at future investment in the southern part of Tolworth

The Broadway may raise its game to accommodate new and expanded shopping needs. The Broadway has been effective at making changes to accommodate new types of residents in our town, and we can expect new changes and more accommodation. In very recent years (2013) there has been a major makeover of the

Broadway in terms of traffic and pedestrian flow, making a link across the by-pass divide for pedestrians and cyclists and providing those road users with space - the Greenway - in place of a set of ugly barriers in the middle of the old Broadway. (There is a photograph of the Greenway making a new path through the centre of Tolworth, on page 125.)

There will be a need for shopping south of the A3 (local to the new housing on the Toby Jug site, and enhancing the town shops), and for places of entertainment, for community facilities, for transportation, for parking, and so on. A market will develop for all of these that will be centred on the south side of the town.

Tolworth Station is located in the midst of all this new development. When the new residents (and the residents in existing homes, particularly as the prosperity of the whole town rises with new development) go looking for access to jobs outside Tolworth, mostly in London, then there will be a rising market for an improved rail service. There is enormous scope for the Tolworth service to rise to a level that offers a realistic alternative to the service from Surbiton Station and there is every chance that it will be met - maybe before the middle of the century. The Cross Rail 2 project, if it goes ahead, will bring a dozen trains a day to Tolworth Station, with fast service into central London, and will liberate railway scheduling from the bottle-neck on traffic into Waterloo that is Clapham Junction.

Road projects also will concentrate attention in the southern part of our town, maybe taming the A3 that has sliced through our town since the 1920s. There is a project proposed (by London Mayor, Boris Johnson) to roof over the underpass and put the A3 in a tunnel. The motivation for this is principally to improve air quality, but it will create new public spaces bridging the divide, and permit greater development (principally of housing) by allowing development near the line of the road. If this project goes ahead, it will also go some way to undoing the division of our town created when the by-pass came in the 1920s.

There is a proposal (from Transport for London) for a flyover that would take traffic from the Broadway straight out towards Ewell on the A240, and *vice versa*. That could pose some challenges for maintaining the Broadway as a place to stroll and shop in peace. But it is undoubtedly another sign of planners seeing the "centre of gravity" within Tolworth itself, and not as an extension of Surbiton.

Other developments in the southern/central parts of Tolworth complement these trends. Tolworth Hospital has been a significant influence on the town since it was opened, as the Isolation Hospital, in 1889. As an NHS hospital, its influence on the town has continued, not least as a source of local employment. The hospital is now part of the South-West London and St. George's Mental Health Trust of the NHS.

This Trust has recently announced a major investment that it is going to make in the Hospital (Surrey Comet 12/09/2014) - more development in the centre of our town.

Currently there is some discussion concerning the future structure of the Church of England locally. It has been suggested that to meet the needs of the influx of new residents, the area south of Red Lion Road would be cut off from St. Matthew's parish and made into a new parish with its own incumbent. Moreover, it is hoped that St Pauls, Hook, will be joined with the two Tolworth parishes, to form a team ministry for Hook and Tolworth. At the time of writing, these plans are in an early stage, but the fact that they are under discussion indicates a local awareness of coming change.

If all this comes about, and the "centre of gravity", as we put it, of Tolworth is restored more to the centre of town what is the significance of that? Our view is that it could have immense significance to Tolworth and some significance in the wider picture of how Greater London operates. This could be nothing less than Tolworth reclaiming itself as a town, a community that will have its own identity and pride, rather than being a rather unassuming southern adjunct to Surbiton. As a separate community, with its own identity, who knows where it will go in terms of developing facilities and life?

Wahid Samady, Chair of CNM, is one man who closely watches the possibilities for development and the way the market is moving. He has been the moving force behind many of the individual developments in the Borough, some of them controversial, some of them imaginative leaps. He is quoted in the Kingston Guardian of 19/3/2015 saying: "People say 'Why are you doing this in Tolworth?' and I say, I am proud that we are doing it in Tolworth. This building is a gateway."

A gateway to Surbiton? A gateway into Kingston Borough? Or a gateway to a newly confident Tolworth standing on its own as a town within Greater London?

This consuming interest in the past and the future which is afforded by a study of our town is likely to be just as interesting in studying many communities that, like ours, are located on the edge of Greater London. Each community, of course, has its own history and is subject to unique pressures of development. But it may be the case that London is surrounded by communities made somewhat anonymous by their subordination to neighbours with better communications and more investment. And it may be the case that some of the communities are, like Tolworth, on the brink of asserting their independent identity.

This observation arises from a result of our study that we did not anticipate at the outset. In writing the story of Tolworth, we arrive at a depiction of a present in which we believe the residents of our town are poised to take ownership of their town in a way that was not really available to the residents of a town that used to be rather contingent on bigger neighbours. This development is important for newcomers, too: when people are new to a town it is a great thing for them to take possession of an independent identity, and stories that tell them the what and where and when of their town.

The study of this history has brought us to these thoughts that are new to us. We would heartily recommend an investment in local history research to anyone else, particularly those who live, like us, on the thriving edge of a great metropolis. The study of history is a path towards discerning those forces that are shaping the future of our communities and their surroundings. It has also been, for us, valuable for the way in which it has caused us to think about the future of the whole of London.

Tolworth Ghosts

The roaring Ace of Spades was A3 biker turf
Close to the north-south two four oh. Today
Commuters think "Home soon" as Tolworth Tower heaves up.
A 60's monument to bad taste, some ingrates say,

Linking the Royal Courts of Hampton and Nonsuch
Forgotten, under the Broadway, runs a phantom route.
Close here, the Hogsmill, way when roads were sloughs
With Tolworth Court as welcome journey's halt.

Before commuter Surbiton or Norbiton arose,
The Court had comprehensive 'ministrating powers
And nearly all about was common land
Til 1830s' closures made it no longer ours

Before the time of contracts - land conveyed -
Great marker trees the lands' bounds over-arched.
And ancient men remembered as small boys,
They were the beaten ones when bounds were marched.

126

by Anna Cunnyngham

Appendix A - The Diversity of Tolworth's Population, 1971-2011

The graph opposite is derived from census data for these 5 decades, for the wards of Surbiton Hill, Tolworth and Hook Rise and Alexandra (2011 and 2001) and for the wards of Surbiton Hill, Tolworth South, Tolworth West and Tolworth East (1991,1981,1971). The statistic used is "Country of Birth" rather than "Ethnicity", because the latter statistic is available only from 1991.

The graph must be taken with a substantial pinch of salt because the country categories used in reporting have changed in every one of these 5 censuses. We have done our best to aggregate data for each census to produce groupings that are fairly comparable across censuses, but this is very difficult to do with complete confidence.

The data was kindly made available by the Kingston Council Data Observatory (thanks to Joyce Wong, Business Analyst in Kingston Data). The wards included were selected by Kingston Data in response to my query about data specifically for Tolworth - we must assume that the boundaries of these wards most closely matches the boundaries of "Tolworth Town". (The question of how to identify these borders in principle is addressed separately in our "Boundaries Appendix", page 131 ff.)

THE STORY OF TOLWORTH

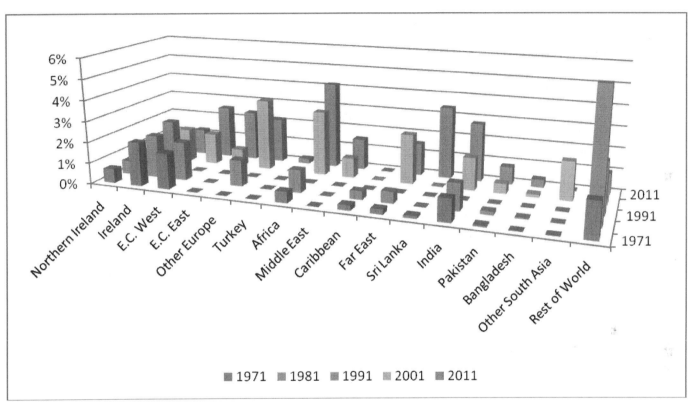

The data from which this graph was drawn is shown in note 87 (pages 173-4)

The figures displayed in the graph are the percentages of the total population of Tolworth represented by each grouping of Country of Birth. The total population of Tolworth over these 5 decades varied as follows: 22,468; 24,178; 21,607; 29,499; 28,748; from 1971 to 2011. Drawing the graph from percentages rather than absolute numbers smoothes out this variation for the purpose of comparison. I have left off the graph the data for Great Britain − at 92%, 85%, 94%, 80%, 76%, this line of data would dominate the graph and make it harder to see the variations in all the other groups.

This line of data − the move from 92% British in 1971 to 76% in 2011 − is of course important, and is the context for the whole of this investigation. Put the other way round, over the course of these 5 decades, the proportion of people living in Tolworth who came from outside Britain rose from 8% to 24% - a three-fold growth. The graph is an attempt to show the more detailed composition of this growth.

Some of the figures that interest us in the analysis (which are represented in the graph) are the following (with a repetition of the caveat that aggregation and exact comparison of this data across censuses is difficult):

- The number of Sri Lankan residents of Tolworth appears to at least treble over the 5 decades, from less than 1% to over 3% (25 to 984). No other group increases its numbers so steeply.

- Eastern Europeans (the group "E.C. East") increase from under 1% to over 2% (from 0 - not counted - to 688; but that number is particularly suspect because the census interest in Eastern Europeans only develops in recent decades: in 2001 Poles are counted as a distinct group; in 2011 Poles, Letts and Romanians are tallied; in earlier decades there is no special interest in Eastern Europe.

- The growth in the numbers from African countries is similarly marked (and also subject to difficulties caused by changes in the classifications over the decades - 1% to 4% 1971-2011 (116 to 1196). One of the difficulties here is that in 1971 and 1981 the census interest was in identifying "New Commonwealth" and "Old Commonwealth" groups of Country of Birth, cutting across continents, but by the 2011 census the Commonwealth has lost its importance as a statistical grouping, and Africa (and other continents) are being sliced up a different way - comparisons are hard to draw from this data.

Appendix B - The Borders of Tolworth

For most of the history of Tolworth, no-one was trying to define borders precisely. Domesday recorded dwellings and land-holdings: it was a list of taxable property, not a map, and there was no effort to draw a line around a hamlet such as Tolworth. The boundaries of a manor like Tolworth Court were important and known. Since those define a part of what is now the southern-most boundary of Tolworth, they are important here, but they only provide a small part of the historical boundary.

Tolworth sat in the middle of common land - even if there might occasionally have been a reason in a particular case to know where the common land began, this did not add up to a need to define the continuous boundary of the community.

With enclosure, which came very late to Tolworth, there did begin to be a need for precise boundaries, but they were boundaries around the newly carved out private land-holdings. Some of these agreements became a part of the eventually defined boundary of the community, but this was not the purpose of the Enclosure Commissioners. If an idea of the boundary of Tolworth was emerging in the 19th century it was as a negative entity

- mostly, that which was not Surbiton. On page 26 of the book we refer to one particularly quaint episode in recalling the boundary of Kingston.

The advent of the Surbiton Improvement Commissioners in 1855 required that a boundary be defined for the newly self-governing area, separate from Kingston. It defined the boundary between Surbiton and part of (north) Tolworth at that point in history, but it did not provide a complete boundary for Tolworth.

Gradually the advance of civilisation, or at least the advance of bureaucracy, incorporated the whole of the British Isles, including our little town, in the machinery of mapping and boundaries. The most commonly accepted boundary lines for any area in Britain are those laid down for the purposes of Local Government, in which the basic unit of community definition is the Ward. At the time of writing, there is a ward called Tolworth and Hook Rise which is the one that most closely corresponds to the area of interest in this book.

The unit of Local Government segmentation, the Ward, is used for a variety of purposes of government, bureaucracy and reporting: it is the basic boundary for enumeration of the Census; it is the basic unit adopted for purposes of collecting and reporting statistics, by the Office of National Statistics and by demographic researchers.

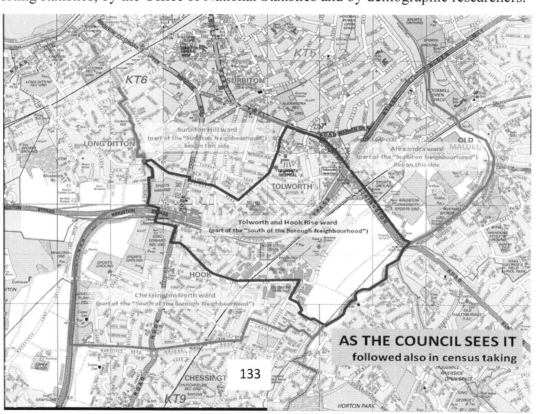

133

It is documented in Ordnance Survey maps.

As in many other parts of Britain, our ward boundaries have shifted over the years; in our case quite recently. We have reported, as a complication in the calculations in Appendix A, that prior to 2000 there were three wards: Tolworth South, West and East. Now there is Tolworth and Hook Rise. But to make up an area corresponding to "Tolworth", for comparison across the years 1971 to 2011, the Kingston Data Observatory (an agency of the Royal Borough of Kingston upon Thames) had to include in a "bundle" of wards Surbiton Hill Ward in the earlier years and Surbiton Hill and Alexandra Wards in the later years. So, although there is, at present, just one ward with Tolworth in its title, that does not, unfortunately, provide us with a definitive boundary that could be said to correspond with our town.

And, the Local Authority is only one body that adjudicates on boundaries, although it is the most authoritative one in modern life. Historically, the Church of England was a potent authority - the boundaries of the parish were t o many people the most salient boundaries (especially in an area of the rural character of Tolworth, before the effects of the railway were felt). The Church of England's definitions of the limits of each parish

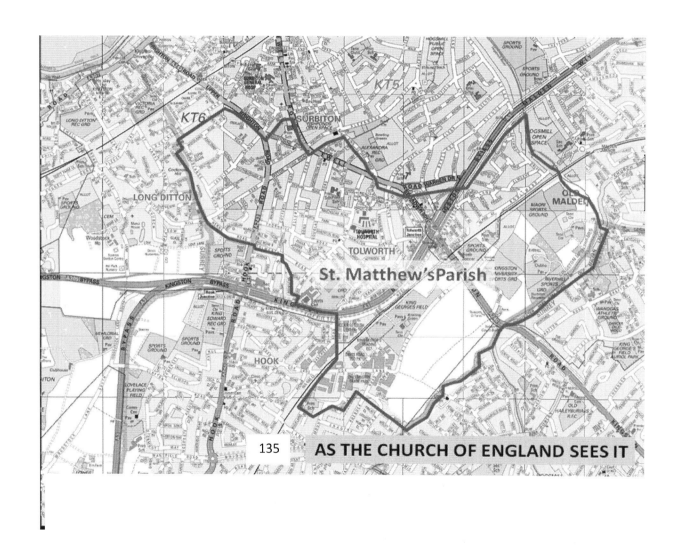

135

AS THE CHURCH OF ENGLAND SEES IT

are still a matter of import, and documented in most general maps. The map on the opposite page shows the boundary of the current Church of England parish that includes Tolworth. As explained in the text of the book (page 122), this parish structure might change relatively soon.

The current boundaries of the parish extend further north and further east than the administrative (ward) boundary - as we will see, the eastern boundary is of particular interest to us as we try to delineate "Tolworth Town".

If we are interested in defining the boundaries of our town, we must take these authorities of Church and State into account, but they do not give us a complete picture. As you would expect from the authors of a book on the history of Tolworth, we believe that there are clues from history that must also be brought into the picture. Even if history does not present us with a neat "boundary package", it does provide us with important indicators. These clues take the form of stretches of boundary that should be incorporated in the overall boundary of Tolworth because these stretches of boundary capture something that history tells us is essential to the identity of "Tolworth Town".

There are places and areas that are crucially important to our history that happen to be located on the periphery of the area of Tolworth. In our view, there are two that cannot be overlooked:

- In the south of Tolworth, Tolworth Court Manor has been for eight centuries the most important location in our town. The southern boundary of the Manor is the Hogsmill River, and it seems without doubt that that section of the Hogsmill should be incorporated in the boundaries drawn for our town.

- Tolworth Brook has always been accepted as the northern border of Tolworth - the boundary between us and the southern limit of Surbiton. In modern times the brook has been straightened and culverted and buried underground in places, and made to run between streets (along Ellerton Road; between Hollyfield and Beaconsfield), but that, in our view, does not rob it of its status as a boundary. There is a question, one might suppose, as to whether the current boundary should be the culverted entrapment of the brook, or its natural line of flow, and also how far the Brook and boundary coincide.

There is evidence for the historical validity of each of these boundaries:

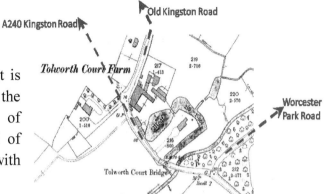

- For the southern segment of boundary that is important to us in this boundary appendix, the clearest piece of evidence is the map of Tolworth Court Manor shown on page 6 of this book, which is copied here, with references to today's road lines.

This map is a bit of an anachronism - it appears in an 1895 Ordnance Survey, from which we have copied it. It is almost certainly the case that the buildings detailed in this map had disappeared before 1895. Nevertheless, it provides a clear illustration of the obvious: that Tolworth Court was a part of our town for a long time prior to 1895. Therefore, the southern boundary of this part of Tolworth must be the Hogsmill River (as it runs today just to the north of Worcester Park Road). Note that this historical piece of Tolworth occupies an area lying to the east of the line of what is now the A240 - east of what is included in the contemporary boundary of Tolworth and Hook Rise Ward.

- For the northern boundary, one question is: how far east along the line of Tolworth Brook does the boundary between Surbiton and Tolworth run?

1888 was the date of publication of Rowley Richardson's history of Surbiton: <u>Surbiton, Thirty-two years of self-government</u>. Richardson was the Chairman of the Surbiton Improvement Commission set up as the administrative authority of Surbiton in 1855. Folded into the cover of this book was a map of Surbiton which gives us an authoritative indication of the boundaries in mid-Victorian times. The southern boundary of Surbiton is, of course, the northern boundary of Tolworth.

A copy of part of Richardson's map is reproduced on the opposite page.
In this map, the boundary follows the Brook eastwards into what is now the Alexandra Recreation area, and then takes a turn southwards across what were then undeveloped fields..

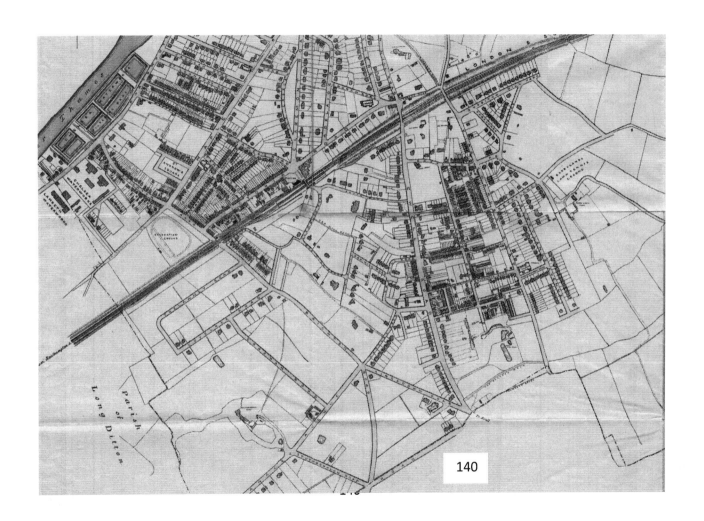

140

The first of these historical clues tells us that the boundary in the south needs to be moved eastwards to include the area of Tolworth Court Manor and Farm. The second tells us that the boundary in the north should run along Tolworth Brook towards the east: it needs to go far enough east to match the first clue. We can sketch these pieces onto our accumulating map of "Tolworth Town":

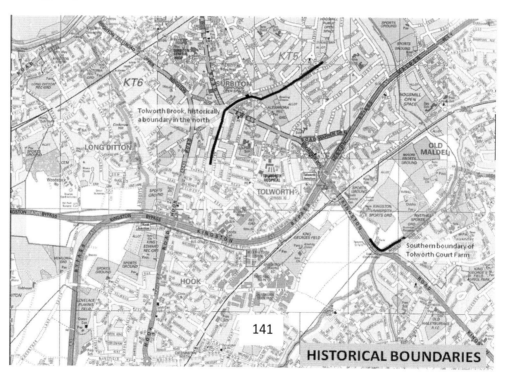

141

HISTORICAL BOUNDARIES

Put those three boundary mapping components (Church, State and History) together, and you get something that is not immediately very useful. The boundaries overlap.

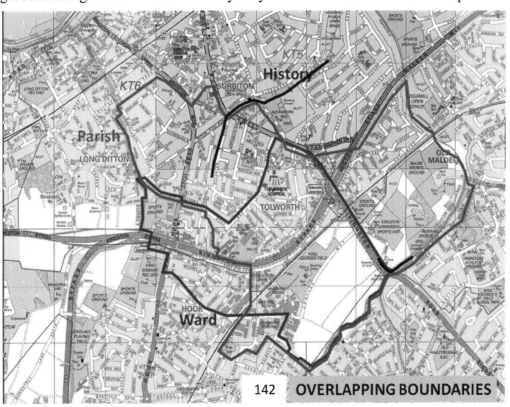

142 OVERLAPPING BOUNDARIES

There are other sources of boundary information. For instance, postal codes are in some circumstances regarded as potent definers of place (as in the phrase: "postal code lottery")

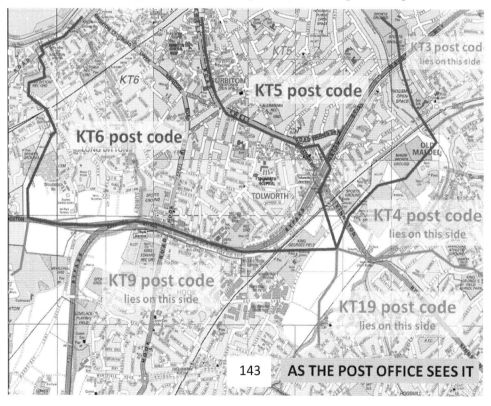

Boundaries do not need to be official to be influential:

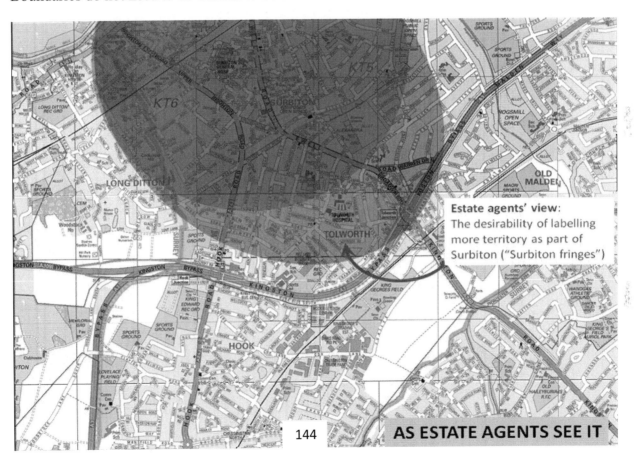

Estate agents' view:
The desirability of labelling more territory as part of Surbiton ("Surbiton fringes")

144

AS ESTATE AGENTS SEE IT

If wut all these points of view together, we create an even bigger confusion:

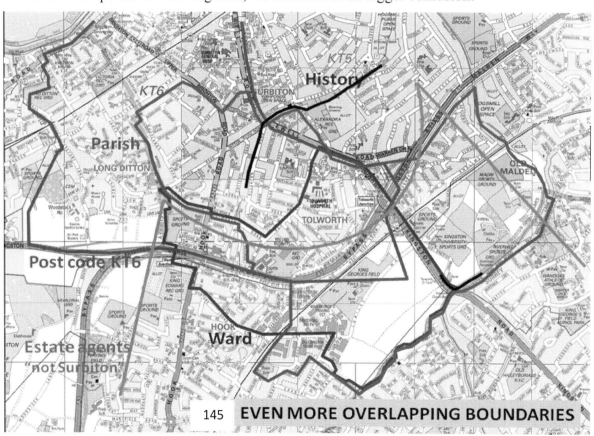

145 EVEN MORE OVERLAPPING BOUNDARIES

In the end, in our view, one has to make a judgement, taking into account many sources of input.

Of course, administrative boundaries as defined by the State are going to govern much of our lives. But if these boundaries do not correspond to the boundaries of a real, living community, then they will not do as the sole authority. The community has to express its own sense of itself. As we have seen, administrative boundaries sometimes change. They change in efforts of bureaucratic tidiness, but they also change because they have to correspond to what people feel about the boundaries of their community.

As historians, we are more than usually sensitive to the notion that people's sense of their community is shaped by history. Even if the people do not know their history, the way that institutions in their town work is determined by historical precedents and forces. The town we live in is partially the town that our forebears handed on to us.

So, our judgement is that the real boundaries of our community are reflected largely in the administrative boundaries given to us, but moderated by reference to history where history is important and where the administrative decisions have cut through really important aspects of our historical, and living, landscape.

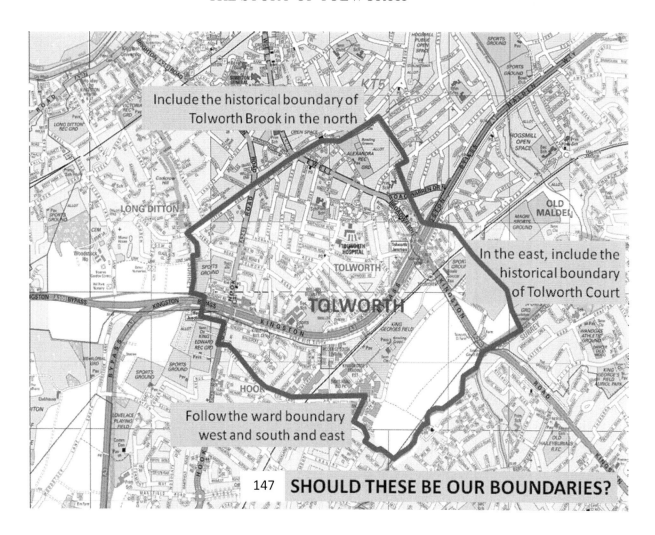

Include the historical boundary of Tolworth Brook in the north

In the east, include the historical boundary of Tolworth Court

Follow the ward boundary west and south and east

147 SHOULD THESE BE OUR BOUNDARIES?

THE STORY OF TOLWORTH

NOTES

We have included two kinds of notes to the main text:

- There are notes for which the intention is to provide justification for something stated in the main text, or a reference, or some other means by which the reader can follow up a point if she or he wishes to;

- There are notes that are intended to provide historical context. It helps in many parts of our story for the reader to know how events in Tolworth fit in with the overall currents of history. For those readers for whom a reminder of that history would be useful, we hope we have included enough in the notes to make the whole story come alive.

  (The text for a number of the general notes is taken, with thanks, from Wikipedia.)

[1] **The Middle Iron Age, and round-houses**

The British Iron Age lasted in theory from the first significant use of iron for tools and weapons in Britain to the Romanisation of the southern half of the island. During the Middle Iron Age the development of hill forts became prevalent; they may have served as wider centres used for markets and social contact. Roman occupation of Britain then came from the 50s BC and marked the end of the British Iron Age and the shift in culture towards the Roman.

The **roundhouse** is a type of house with a circular plan, originally built in western Europe, using walls made of stone or wooden posts joined by wattle-and-daub panels, and a conical thatched roof. Roundhouses ranged in size from less than 5m in diameter to over 15m.

[2] **The Domesday Book**

The Domesday Book is a manuscript record of the "Great Survey" of much of England and parts of Wales completed in 1086 by order of King William the Conqueror. The survey's main purpose was to determine what taxes had been owed during the reign of King Edward the Confessor.

[3] John Blair, Medieval Surrey: Landholding, Church and Settlement Before 1300, Sutton, 1990

[4] **Kingston Hundred**

The "Hundred" was the division of a shire for military and judicial purposes under the common law. When introduced by the Saxons between 613 and 1017, a hundred had land which sustained approximately 100 households, defined as the land covered by one hundred hides.

[5] **The Lord of the Manor**

The Manor was the pivot of the feudal system - embodying the theory that human society was divided into three orders, the *oratores*, the *bellatores*, and the *laboratores*: those who protected (the Kingdom) with their prayers, those who used their swords, and those who tilled the earth to support the other two classes. By the time of Edward the Confessor (r 1042-66), the Lord of the Manor was the most important person in village affairs, collecting taxes for the King or dispensing justice.

[6] **The Norman Conquest**

The Norman conquest of England was the 11th-century invasion and occupation of England by an army of Norman, Breton, and French soldiers led by Duke William II of Normandy, later known as William the Conqueror. This was a pivotal event in English history. It largely removed the native ruling class, replacing it with a foreign, French-speaking monarchy, aristocracy, and clerical hierarchy. This, in turn, brought about a transformation of the English language and the culture of England in a new era.

[7] Rebecca Hughes, "Tolworth, Surrey: medieval settlement", 2014

[8] Serjeants' Accounts, 1398-1481, National Archives, Kew

[9] Alfred Heales, The Records of Merton Priory in the County of Surrey, Henry Frowde, 1898

[10] **Merton Priory**

Merton Priory was founded in 1114 by Gilbert Norman, Sheriff of Surrey under Henry I. It was located in Merton, Surrey at the point where the Roman Stane Street crossed the River Wandle. By 1117 the foundation had been colonised by Canons Regular from the Augustinian Priory at Huntingdon. The priory became distinguished as an important centre of learning, and the location of what is arguably the first Parliament, held there under Henry II in 1236, at which the Statute of Merton was agreed allowing amongst other matters Lords of the Manor to enclose common land provided that sufficient pasture remained for their tenants.

[11] **The Despensers**

Hugh Despenser, 1st Lord Despenser (c. 1286 -1326), also referred to as "the younger Despenser", was the son and heir of Hugh le Despenser, Earl of Winchester (the elder Despenser), and Isabella daughter of William, 9th Earl of Warwick. He rose to national prominence as royal chamberlain and a favourite of Edward II of England. A series of subsequent controversies eventually led to his being hanged, drawn and quartered.

[12] **Edward II's Palace at Sheen**

This Palace was erected at Sheen about 1501 by Henry VII, formerly known as *Earl of Richmond*, in honour of which the manor of Sheen had recently been renamed as "Richmond". It replaced a former palace, itself built on the site of a manor house appropriated by the Crown some two centuries before. Edward II used this Palace frequently, meeting Eleanor Despenser (his niece, Hugh's wife) there several times.

[13] Brayley, page 298

[14] Stewards' Memoranda Book, 1802-09, University of Sussex, Archaeological library

[15] "**Brayest Mulne**"

"Mulne" may be a reference to a mill, but the meaning of this phrase is obscure. Also "a building for turning carts" may refer simply to a barn with two openings for a cart.

[16] Tolworth Court Farm dig report, 2000, Kingston upon Thames Archaeological Society

[17] **John Blair**

His book Early Medieval Surrey: Landholding, Church and Settlement Before 1300, 1990, Sutton Publishing Ltd., is the definitive history of Surrey at this time.

[18] Hughes, 2014

[19] **Baron's Court**

The main business of the Court Baron was the resolution of disputes involving a lord's free tenants within a single manor, to enforce the feudal services owed to the lord of the manor by his tenants, and to admit new tenants who had acquired copyholds by inheritance or purchase, for which they were obliged to pay a fine to the lord of the manor.

[20] **A tithing of Ewell**

A tithing or tything was an historic English legal, administrative or territorial unit, originally one tenth of a hundred, and later a subdivision of a manor or civil parish. It implies a grouping of ten households.

[21] **Pannage**

Pannage is the practice of releasing domestic pigs in a forest, in order that they may feed on fallen acorns, beechmast, chestnuts or other nuts. Historically, it was a right or privilege granted to local people on common land or in royal forests.

[22] Blair, page 82

[23] Tolworth Court Farm dig report, 2000, Kingston upon Thames Archaeological Society

[24] **Black Death**

The Black Death was one of the most devastating pandemics in human history, resulting in the deaths of an estimated 75 to 200 million people and peaking in Europe in the years 1346–53. The pathogen responsible was almost certainly the *yersinia pestis* bacterium, causing several forms of plague.

[25] **Minster**

"Minster" could apply to any church whose clergy followed a formal rule: as for example a monastery or a chapter; or to a church served by a less formal group of clergy living communally. By the 11th century, a hierarchy of minster churches became apparent; cathedral churches, or *head minsters* having pre-eminence within a diocese; *old minsters* being pre-eminent within an area broadly equiv-alent to an administrative hundred. The minster church for Kingston Hundred was All Souls, Kingston.

[26] Blair, page 105

[27] **The Augustinians**

The religious orders of the Augustinians (named after Saint Augustine of Hippo), include various congregations of clerics, known as canons regular, who are priests living in community under the Rule of St. Augustine ("regula" in Latin), and sharing their property in common. The order has some similarity to a monastic order, living a cloistered, contemplative life and sometimes engaging in ministry to those from outside the monastery, but the purpose of the life of a canon is to engage in public ministry of liturgy and sacraments for those who visit their churches..

[28] Blair, page 99

[29] **The Norman religious revival**
This 11-12th century religious revival was strongly promoted by the Norman rulers of England. Evidence for the revival can be found in the First Crusade, and also in the many Norman churches built in southern England.

[30] Blair, page 101

[31] **The Priory at Lewes**
The Priory of St Pancras was the first Cluniac house in England and had one of the largest monastic churches in the country. The motherhouse of the Congregation of Cluny was the Benedictine Abbey of Cluny. The Priory was set within an extensive walled and gated precinct laid out in a commanding location fronting the tidal shore-line at the head of the Ouse valley to the south of Lewes in the County of Sussex.

[32] Blair, page 99

[33] Record of Merton Priory

[34] Tolworth Court Farm dig report, 2000, Kingston upon Thames Archaeological Society

[35] The feudal system

Feudalism is a grouping of legal and military customs which flourished between the 9th and 15th centuries: a system for structuring society around relationships derived from the holding of land in exchange for service or labour. The feudal system of land tenure could be either free-hold, signifying that they were hereditable or perpetual, or non-free where the tenancy terminated on the tenant's death or at an earlier specified period.

One form, "serjeanty", gave tenure in return for acting as a servant to the king, in a non-military capacity. In another form, by "fee-farm", a grant of the right to collect and retain revenues was given in return for a fixed rent. In tenure by "copyhold" the duties and obligations were tailored to the requirements of the lord of the manor and a copy of the terms agreed was entered on the roll of the manorial court as a record. There was form of tenure, "socage", involving payment in produce or in money, and there was tenure by "quit-rent" in which an annual fee was paid in exchange for freedom from all other feudal obligations.

[36] The Reformation

The English Reformation was a series of events in 16th century England by which the Church of England broke away from the authority of the Pope and the Catholic Church.

These events were, in part, associated with the wider process of the European Protestant Reformation, a religious and political movement that affected the practice of Christianity across most of Europe during this period. Many factors contributed to the process: the decline of feudalism and the rise of nationalism, the rise of the common law, the invention of the printing press and increased circulation of the Bible, the transmission of new knowledge and ideas among scholars, the upper and middle classes and readers in general. However, the various phases of the English Reformation, which also covered Wales and Ireland, were largely driven by changes in government policy, to which public opinion gradually accommodated itself.

Based on Henry VIII's desire for an annulment of his marriage (first requested of Pope Clement VII in 1527), the English Reformation was at the outset more of a political affair than a theological dispute. The break with Rome was effected by a series of acts of Parliament passed between 1532 and 1534, among them the 1534 Act of Supremacy which declared that Henry was the "Supreme Head on earth of the Church of England".

[37] The Dissolution of the Monasteries
The Dissolution of the Monasteries was the set of administrative and legal processes between 1536 and 1541 by which Henry VIII disbanded monasteries, priories, convents and friaries in England, Wales and Ireland, appropriated their income, disposed of their assets, and provided for their former members and functions. Since the reign of William the Conqueror, all land in Britain was legally the possession of the

monarch, so Henry conceived his action as the return of the land of the monasteries to their rightful ownership.

[38] Brayley, page 298

[39] Brayley, page 298

[40] Information about Nathaniel Polhill has been gained principally from the papers <u>Lands in the Manor of Talworth</u>, held in the National Archives, Kew

[41] <u>Pubs, Inns and Taverns of Surbiton and Malden</u>, Richard F. Holmes

[42] **Common land**
In medieval England the common was an integral part of the manor, and was thus legally part of the estate owned by the lord of the manor, but over which certain classes of manorial tenants and others held certain rights. The ownership of most "appurtenant" rights belonged to tenancies of particular plots of land held within a manor. A commoner would be the person who, for the time being, was the occupier of a particular plot of land. Some rights of common were said to be "in gross", that is, they were unconnected with tenure of land. This included many village greens across England and Wales. Most land with appurtenant commons rights is adjacent to the common or even surrounded by it.

[43] Stewards' Memoranda

[44] Stewards' Memoranda

[45] Surveyors' Highway Book, 1841, held at the Surrey Local History Centre, Woking

[46] **Hampton Court Palace**
The Palace was originally built for Cardinal Thomas Wolsey, a favourite of King Henry VIII, circa 1514. In 1529, as Wolsey fell from favour, the palace was passed to King Henry VIII, who enlarged it. In the following century, William III undertook a massive rebuilding and expansion project intended to rival Versailles, but work on this project halted in 1694.

[47] **Nonsuch Palace**
Nonsuch Palace was perhaps the grandest of Henry VIII's building projects. It was built on the site of Cuddington, near Ewell, the church and village having been destroyed and compensation paid to create a suitable site. The palace was designed to be a celebration of the power and the grandeur of the Tudor dynasty, built to rival Francis I's Château de Chambord. Unlike most of Henry's palaces, Nonsuch was not an adaptation of an old building; he chose to build a new palace in this location because it was near to one of his main hunting grounds.

The palace was incomplete when Henry VIII died in 1547. In 1556 Queen Mary I sold it to the 19th Earl of Arundel who completed it. It returned to royal hands in the 1590s, and remained royal property until 1670, when Charles II gave it to his mistress, Barbara, Countess of Castlemaine. She had it pulled down around 1682–3 and sold off the building materials to pay gambling debts.

[48] Green wood, page 50

[49] **Enclosure**
The Tolworth Enclosure Act repeated a pattern of change that had started in other parts of the English countryside more than a hundred years previously. It is the process which ends traditional rights such as mowing meadows for hay, or grazing livestock on common land formerly held in the open field system. Once enclosed, these uses of the land become restricted to the owner, and it ceases to be land for commons. In England and Wales the term is also used for the process that ended the ancient system of arable farming in open fields. Under enclosure, such land is fenced (enclosed) and deeded or entitled to one or more owners.

[50] Manor of Tolworth; Book of Plans, held at the Surrey Local History Centre, Woking

[51] Stewards' Memoranda

[52] A donation of £24,000 in 1875

This is equivalent to some £16m in 2014 - using the "economic status value" calculation from MeasuringWorth.com.   MeasuringWorth is not incorporated or directly connected to any institution, but has a Board of Advisors from universities such as Oxford, Harvard, LSE, etc. This service applies alternative monetary scales or indicators from the desired (later or present) year to an item in the initial (past) year. The result is a value that has been adjusted (usually increased) by the growth in the indicator. Economic status value, in particular, measures a subject (income or wealth) relative to a wage or more general income, such as the wage rate of workers in manufacturing or per-capita GDP.

[53] Sampson, page 30; Butters, pages 210-215

[54] The demise of Thomas Pooley

It could be argued that Thomas Pooley was the first town planner in England, although that accolade is given to Ebenezer Howard in all the textbooks. But Pooley's imaginative venture - he was the first person to recognise the importance of railway commuting to town planning, and to act on it - came to nothing when his bankers brought him to penury and to die a pauper. His memorial is the town of Surbiton, built exactly as he laid it out, but with the profits going to Coutts Bank.

[55] Coutts Bank's investment venture in Surbiton

Edna Healey, in Coutts & Co: The Portrait of a Private Bank, (Hodder & Stoughton, 1992), page 300 writes: "The march of progress also brought prosperity to the banking world and that prosperity made Angela

[Burdett-Coutts (1814-1906)]'s generosity possible. In Thomas [Coutts - the man (1761-1822) who shaped Coutts Banks during its rise]'s day, the Bank had made few investments, because he himself was extremely cautious. Now there was spare capital and a new home for it in the expanding industries. The spread of railways at home and abroad attracted speculators. Fortunes could be made and lost on the railroads and Coutts' customers were among the many who took the gamble.

One of the interesting results of the boom in railway expansion which was to involve Coutts & Co. closely was the development of the town of Surbiton.1t is a good example of the drive and energy in Victorian England."

[56] Brown, page 3

[57] **The Clapham Sect**
This was a group of influential like-minded Church of England social reformers based in Clapham, London at the beginning of the 19th century (active c. 1790–1830). They are described by the historian Stephen Tomkins as "a network of friends and families in England, with William Wilberforce as its centre of gravity, who were powerfully bound together by their shared moral and spiritual values, by their religious mission and social activism, by their love for each other, and by marriage".

[58] Healey, page 354

[59] Millais' Ophelia

The young lady who "sat" for the figure of Ophelia in this painting was Elizabeth Siddal, then only 19 years of age but moving into her life as painter and the muse of the Pre-Raphaelite brotherhood. John Everett Millais and his friend William Holman Hunt both used the scenery of the Hogsmill River as the background for paintings. (In Holman Hunt's case "The Light of the World" and "The Hireling Shepherd".) The name "Hogsmill River", being less than euphonious, was not included in the titles of any of their works. Sad.

Millais and Holman Hunt lodged on Surbiton Hill (so, almost in Tolowrth) while Millais was working on the painting - 1851-52. (See June Sampson's article, " A brush with the Pre-Raphaelites".)

[60] Orders in Council

St. Matthew's parish was created by Orders in Council in 1876. An Order in Council is a type of legislation formally made in the name of the monarch by the Privy Council (King- or Queen-in-Council).

Although the Orders are officially made by the monarch, in practice, royal assent is a formality only. What actually happens is that a representative of the government (generally a cabinet minister or the Lord President of the Council) reads out batches of Orders in Council drafted by the government in front of the monarch, who, after each order, says "Approved". They then come into effect.

[61] Surbiton Improvement Commissioners

Boards of improvement commissioners were ad hoc urban local government boards created during the 18th and 19th centuries in the United Kingdom. Around 300 boards were created, each by a private Act of Parliament, typically termed an Improvement Act. The powers of the boards varied according to the acts which created them. They often included street paving, cleansing, lighting, providing watchmen or dealing with various public nuisances

[62] Vestry

The Vestry meeting is part of the governance of a Church of England parish. That is still true today, but in Victorian times, the Vestry meeting wielded considerable power. In England, until the 19th century, the parish vestry was in effect what would today usually be called a parochial church council, but were also responsible for all the secular parish business. Records of parish business would be stored in a "parish chest" kept in the church and provided for security with three locks, the keys to which would be held by the incumbent and the churchwardens.

[63] St Pauls, Hook

The third parish that may be joined with St. Matthew's parish and a new St. George's, Tolworth, parish to form three parts of a Team Ministry in a reorganisation of the Church of England in this locality under consideration at the time this book is being published..

[64] Parish Magazine

The example given of the contents of a Parish Magazine is dated by the item "John Bright, *In Memoriam*". John Bright, Parliamentary Radical and orator, Quaker and famous for opposing the Corn Laws, died on 27th March 1889.

[65] Church Missionary Society

The Church Mission Society, also known as the Church Missionary Society (CMS), is a group of evangelistic societies working with the Anglican Communion and Protestant Christians around the world. Founded in 1799, CMS has attracted over nine thousand men and women to serve as mission partners during its 200-year history.

[66] Tithe rent redemption

The tithe was originally paid by the tenant as 10% of the rent for the Church of England clergy. In 1891, this became payable by the land-owner. At the time of the second Southborough auction (1882) the payment seems to have been commuted to a sum of 10% of the purchase price.

[67] The Austro-Hungarian Empire and the rule of Habsburgs

This was a constitutional union of the Empire of Austria and the Kingdom of Hungary that existed from 1867 to 1918, when it collapsed as a result of defeat in World War I. It was ruled by the House of Habsburg, and constituted the last phase in the constitutional evolution of the Habsburg Monarchy.

Following reforms in 1867, the Austrian and the Hungarian states were co-equal within the Empire. Austria-Hungary was a multinational realm and one of the world's great powers. It was geographically the second-largest country in Europe after the Russian Empire.

[68] Russia

For 3½ centuries the Tsar was the supreme ruler of Russia, easily the biggest nation in Europe (or maybe not just Europe, but positioned between Europe and Asia). The first Tsar in the Romanov dynasty (Michael I) took the throne in 1613; the last Romanov Tsar (Nicholas II) died in 1917, followed the Bolshevik Revolution in Russia.

[69] The Influenza Epidemic of 1918-19

As the world extricated itself from the devastating World War, an influenza or flu pandemic, the deadliest in modern history, infected an estimated 500 million people worldwide–about one-third of the planet's population at the time–and killed an estimated 20 million to 50 million victims. It was bigger killer than the War had been. The 1918 flu was first observed in Europe, the U.S. and parts of Asia before swiftly spreading around the world. Surprisingly, many flu victims were young, otherwise healthy adults.

[70] The End of World War I

The armistice between the Allies and Germany – known as the Armistice of Compiègne after the location in which it was signed – was the agreement that ended the fighting in western Europe that comprised the First World War. The armistice marked the cessation of hostilities - the precursor to the negotiation of peace terms. The armistice went into effect at 11 a.m. Paris time on November 11, 1918, and marked a victory for the Allies and a complete defeat for Germany, although not formally a surrender.

[71] The Boy Scouts

The Boy Scouts Association was formed in 1910. There had been in the preceding years a rapidly growing number of Scout Patrols, which had begun to form spontaneously following the publication of <u>Scouting for Boys</u> in 1908, written by Lieutenant-General Robert Baden-Powel who became the World Chief Scout.

[72] Building Societies

A building society is a financial institution owned by its members as a mutual organisation. (A mutual is owned by, and run for the benefit of, its members - it has no external shareholders.) Building societies offer banking and related financial services, especially savings and mortgage lending. The term "building society" first arose in the 18th century in Great Britain from cooperative savings groups. In the UK today, building societies compete with banks for most consumer banking services, especially mortgage lending and savings accounts.

[73] Phoney War

The **Phoney War** was a phase early in World War II that was marked by a lack of major military operations by the Western Allies (the United Kingdom and France) against the German Reich. The phase covered the months following Britain's and France's declaration of war on Germany (shortly after the Invasion of

Poland) in September 1939 and preceding the Battle of France in May 1940. War was declared by each side, but no Western power committed to launching a significant land offensive.

[74] Festival of Britain

The **Festival of Britain** was a national exhibition held throughout the United Kingdom in the summer of 1951. It was organised by the government to give the British a feeling of recovery in the aftermath of war and to promote the British contribution to science, technology, industrial design, architecture and the arts. The Festival's centrepiece was in London on the South Bank of the Thames.

[75] Grass courts dug up for allotments

"1939-45 - the Club remained open throughout the war, thanks almost entirely to the efforts of Mr. Leslie Perry, the Honorary Secretary at the time. The lower grass courts were dug up for allotments." From the Club's web site: www.surbiton.org - History of the Club.

[76] Alias David Bowie, Peter and Leni Gillman, New English Library Ltd, 1987

[77] "almost despite itself"

The fact that in 1966 John Lennon's father Freddie was one of the staff at the Toby Jug may go a little way to explaining its ability to identify and pull acts that became so big. See Tolworth Remembered, Mark Davison & Paul Adams, page 62.

[78] **1932 Pathé newsreel:** https://www.youtube.com/watch?v=vWhslVtdXG8#t=50

[79] **Posting on bulletin board:** http://www.surbiton.com/forum/ace-spades-history

[80] **Flight magazine, July 6, 1933, page 672**

[81] **By-pass bikers**
It is unclear whether the photograph included here is of one of the Tip-Top Café motorcyclists. There does exist a photograph of the genuine article, including one of the few women bikers. Unfortunately, that photograph is in the control of Getty Images Ltd., and the price asked for using it is beyond our budget. But you can look at that photo at:
http://www.gettyimages.co.uk/search/2/image?family=editorial&phrase=%22riverhill+riders%22&excludenudity=true

I believe that the young woman in the photo is called Jaqueline - see "Anthony's"posts at
http://www.surbiton.com/forum/ace-spades-history

82 Alexandra Park and the northern boundary of Tolworth

Alexandra Park is legitimately included in Tolworth, the traditional northern boundary of which is the Tolworth Brook running beside Hollyfield Road. (Appendix B provides further discussion of this and the other boundaries of Tolworth.) This map shows the brook today, thoroughly contained in a culvert as it passes through this part of town.

see the map opposite

Most of Alexandra Park is south of the Brook, even in its culvert. If the boundary is held to be the natural line of flow of the Brook, then even the distinguished Surrey Croquet Club could be deemed to be within the boundaries of Tolworth, and for the purposes of this book we will generously give them that honour. I guess we have no expectation any time soon of a name change to have the most prestigious international croquet tournaments played at the Tolworth Croquet Club.

83 The MacRobertson International Croquet Shield

This is the premier event in the world for croquet teams. It is currently competed for by Australia, England, New Zealand and the United States. It is known affectionately as the MacRob or just the Mac. and the match in the photograph, being played at the Surbiton Croquet Club in 2010, was against Australia

[84] **National Health Service**

The four publicly funded health care systems in the four countries of the United Kingdom are referred to as the National Health omprehensive range of Service (NHS). The systems are primarily funded through central taxation. They provide a comprehensive range of health services, the vast majority of which are free at the point of use for people legally resident in the United Kingdom. The systems are primarily funded through central taxation. They provide a chealth services, the vast majority of which are free at the point of use for people legally resident in the United Kingdom.

[85] **Windsor Laundry workforce**

See Ward, page 24; and Davison and Adams, page 23

[86] See chapter 1 "An entrepreneurial wizard" in the book The Picker House and Collection, Jonathan Black *et al*.

[87] **Country of Birth histogram**

We have shown on the opposite page the data from which the 3D histogram in appendix A was derived. Bear in mind the *caveats* given in that appendix - this data is consolidated from 5 decades of census data in which the country categories employed have changed from census to census.

	1971	1981	1991	2001	2011
Northern Ireland	1%	1%	1%	1%	0%
Ireland	2%	2%	2%	2%	1%
E.C. West	2%	2%	0%	2%	3%
E.C. East	0%	0%	0%	1%	2%
Other Europe	0%	1%	0%	3%	2%
Turkey	0%	0%	0%	0%	0%
Africa	1%	1%	0%	3%	4%
Middle East	0%	0%	0%	1%	1%
Caribbean	0%	0%	0%	0%	0%
Far East	0%	1%	0%	2%	2%
Sri Lanka	0%	0%	0%	0%	3%
India	1%	1%	0%	2%	3%
Pakistan	0%	0%	0%	0%	1%
Bangladesh	0%	0%	0%	0%	0%
Other South Asia	0%	0%	0%	2%	0%
Rest of World	2%	6%	2%	0%	1%

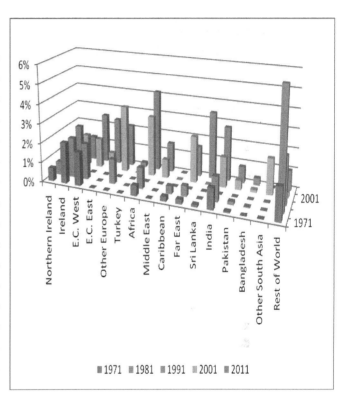

ILLUSTRATIONS

The following is a list of all the illustrations used in this book, with sources and copyright information.

page	Illustration	Origin	Publisher/Source	Web Site / Email
0	1816 map and modern aerial photograph	OS One Inch (1:63,360), First Series, Surrey Sheet XIII, 1816 and photograph in Kingston Archives	Ordnance Survey, and Kingston Museum and Heritage Service	local.history@rbk.kingston.gov.uk
1	A medieval ploughman	Miniature in an Anglo Saxon manuscript published by Shaw	Wikipedia Commons	https://commons.wikimedia.org/wiki
2	Reconstruction of an Iron Age settlement at New Malden, c. 300	Kingston Museum, photographed by Les Kirkin	Kingston Museum and Heritage Service	local.history@rbk.kingston.gov.uk

page	Illustration	Origin	Publisher/Source	Web Site / Email	
3	King Henry I of England	from Cassell's History of England, Century Edition, 1902	Wikipedia Commons	https://commons.wiki media.org/wiki	
4	The escutcheon of the Picot family	Escutcheon of the Family of Picot	House of Names	www.houseofnames .com	with kind per-mission from the House of Names
5	Edward II of England receiving his crown	from the Chronicle of England, circe 1315	Wikipedia Commons	https://commons. wikimedia.org/wiki	
6	Outline plan of Tolworth Court	OS Six Inch (1:10,560), 1888-1913 Series, Surrey Sheet XIII, 1895	Ordnance Survey		
7	Hampton Court and Gardens	drawn and engraved by Knyff for *Britannia illustrata* (1708)	Wikipedia Commons	https://commons. wikimedia.org/wiki	

page	Illustration	Origin	Publisher/Source	Web Site / Email	
7	Nonsuch Palace from the north-east	attributed to Hendrick Danckerts, circa 1666–1679	Wikipedia Commons	https://commons. wikimedia.org/wiki	
8	Tolworth Court in the Map of Surrey, 1596	Collection: 250 years of map making in the County of Surrey	Philllimore & Co.		
9	Croydon Palace	from The Antiquities of England and Wales, first published in 1772/3	Wikipedia Commons	https://commons. wikimedia.org/wiki	
10	Mediaeval livestock - woodcut	woodcut, Thuróczy Chronicle, Brno edition, 1488	Wikipedia Commons	https://commons. wikimedia.org/wiki	
11	Artist's impression of medieval woodland in use	Illustration for Chiltern Conservation	Richard Allen, artist	www.richardallenillustrator.com	with kind permission of Richard Allen

page	Illustration	Origin	Publisher/Source	Web Site / Email	
12	The Black Death	from the Toggenburg Bible, 1411	Wikipedia Commons	https://commons. wikimedia.org/wiki	
13	12th century wall at St. Mary's Church, Long Ditton		photograph taken for this book		kindly taken by Derek Winterburn
14	12th century arch at Merton Priory, excavated and reconstructed	Archaeology at Abbey House site	David Saxby, archaeologist		with kind permission of David Saxby
15	Map locating Bletchingley	Google maps	Google maps		
17	Henry VIII, circa 1540	by the workshop of Hans Holbein the Younger 1537-47	Wikipedia Commons	https://commons. wikimedia.org/wiki	

page	Illustration	Origin	Publisher/Source	Web Site / Email	
18	John Evelyn at 28	by Robert Walker, 1648	Wikipedia Commons	https://commons. wikimedia.org/wiki	
20	Tolworth in the first series of OS maps, 1816	OS One Inch (1:63,360), First Series, Surrey Sheet XIII, 1816	Ordnance Survey		
21	Map - the strip separating Long Ditton and Tolworth Parish	The Story of 'Hook in Kingston', Marion C. Bone	The Parochial Church Council of St. Paul, Hook		with kind permission of Marion Bone
22	A blacksmith in Victorian times	The Village Farrier by Eyre Crowe, 1903 oil painting	Kathryn Summerwill, archivist of Eyre Crowe	http://eyrecrowe.com	with kind permission of Kathryn Summerwill
23	The Royal Oak public house		photograph taken for this book		kindly taken by Derek Winterburn

page	Illustration	Origin	Publisher/Source	Web Site / Email	
23	The Red Lion public house	Photograph contributed by Colin Smith	The Geograph® Britain and Ireland project		Licensed under a Creative Commons Licence
24	Page 1 of the "Act for Dividing and Inclosing certain Common Fields in the Hamlet of Shipton, 1745"	Shipton Enclosure Award 29 April 1745	Winslow History Project	www.winslow-history.org	with kind permission of Julian Hunt
26	Beating the Bounds	cited in The Frontier blog	Charlotte Street project	www.charlottestreet.org	
27	Queen Victoria in 1887	Photograph of Queen Victoria dressed for the wedding of The Duke and Duchess of Albany, by Alexander Bassano	Wikipedia Commons	https://commons.wikimedia.org/wiki	
28	Route of the railway through Surbiton	The London and Southampton Railway Guide, 1839, pub James Wyld	Hampshire Map Catalogue - Martin Northgate	www.geog.port.ac.uk/webmap/hantscat/	with kind permission of Martin Norgate

page	Illustration	Origin	Publisher/Source	Web Site / Email	
29	Old Surbiton Railway Station, 1938	Kingston photograph collection K2-1379	Kingston Museum and Heritage Service	local.history@rbk. kingston.gov.uk	
30	Surbiton Railway Station today (view of Glenbuck Road entrance)	Collection of photographs of Surbiton Station	Shadow in the Water	flickr.com	with kind permission of Carole King
32	Map of Tolworth, 1866	OS Six Inch (1:10,560), Old Series, Surrey Sheet XIII, 1867, pub.1871	Ordnance Survey		
33	Immanuel Church, Streatham	Parish web site home page	Parish Church Council of Immanuel and St Andrew, Streatham		with kind permission of David Gray of Immanuel
34	The Clapham Sect	cited in article: Clapham: A Missional Community	New Zealand Christian Network	www.nzchristian network.	

page	Illustration	Origin	Publisher/Source	Web Site / Email	
35	Plaque in memory of Mabella, William Coulthurst's sister	London Churches in Photographs	Andrew Wood	https://londonchurch buildings.wordpress .com	with kind permission of Andrew Wood
36	St Matthew's Church, Tolworth Parish	Mary Platford, NDD	From Talworth Hamlet to Tolworth Tower		with kind permission of the late Mary Platford
37	Ophelia, painted by Millais	Reproduction of the painting in	Tate Britain	http://en.wikipedia .org/wiki/Ophelia	
38	Rev TC Griffiths	Framed photograph in St. Matthew's Church	St. Matthew's Parish Council		with kind permission of St. Matthew's PCC
40	Map of St Matthew's Parish	Church of England	List of parishes	www.achurchnearyou .com	

page	Illustration	Origin	Publisher/Source	Web Site / Email	
42	Hipwell cottages, Red Lion Road	Mary Platford, NDD	From Talworth Hamlet to Tolworth Tower		with kind permission of the late Mary Platford
43	Parish Magazine contents		St. Matthew's parish magazine		Reproduced by permission of Surrey History Centre
44	"The Mission House and party, and the Wa-Taita natives"	Church Missionary Society	St. Matthew's parish magazine		Reproduced by permission of Surrey History Centre
45	The St. Matthew's Parish school house	Mary Platford, NDD	From Talworth Hamlet to Tolworth Tower		with kind permission of the late Mary Platford
46	The first St. Matthew's school building, in 2013		LISC		with kind permission of LISC Independent Tutorial College

page	Illustration	Origin	Publisher/Source	Web Site / Email	
48	Map of Tolworth, 1896	OS Six Inch (1:10,560), 1888-1913 Series, Surrey Sheet XIII, 1895, pub. 1898	Ordnance Survey		
49	Site of the Pyne Road Mission Hall		photograph taken for this book		taken by Bob Phillips
50	Pyne Road		photograph taken for this book		taken by Bob Phillips
51	St. Matthew's Church, Tolworth Parish	London Churches in Photographs	Andrew Wood	https://londonchurchbuildings.wordpress.com	with kind permission of Andrew Wood
52	Graph of population of Tolworth	Census data assembled by Brian Hawksbee	Bob Phillips		

page	Illustration	Origin	Publisher/Source	Web Site / Email
53	Southbrough Lodge	Painting by John Bray, 1966, a winner in the Brill Competition	Brill Collection, Kingston Museum	southborough-residents.org
53	The Southborugh Estate and environs in 1867	Painting by John Bray, 1966, a winner in the Brill Competition	Ordnance Survey	
54	The Southborugh Estate and environs in 1895	OS Six Inch (1:10,560), 1888-1913 Series, Surrey Sheet XIII, 1895, pub. 1898	Ordnance Survey	
55	William Ewart Gladstone, circa 1890	photographed bt the London Stereoscopic Company	Wikipedia Commons	https://commons. wikimedia.org/wiki
56	Original door at the Isolation Hospital in Red Lion Road		photograph taken for this book	kindly taken by Derek Winterburn

page	Illustration	Origin	Publisher/Source	Web Site / Email
57	Facsimile of letters page, 4/12/1880	Reconstruction from the columns of The Surrey Comet	Kingston Museum and Heritage Service	
59	1894 Local Government Act, page 1	Reconstruction from archives	HM Government	www.legislation .gov.uk
60	The offices of Surbiton Urban District Council, Ewell Rd, 1931	Kingston photograph collection K2-113	Kingston Museum and Heritage Service	local.history@rbk .kingston.gov.uk
61	Houses in Worthington Road built in the 1880s		photograph taken for this book	kindly taken by Derek Winterburn
62	Opening of Tolworth Fountain, Royal Oak, Ewell Road, July 1901	Kingston photograph collection K2-1039	Kingston Museum and Heritage Service	local.history@rbk .kingston.gov.uk

page	Illustration	Origin	Publisher/Source	Web Site / Email	
63	Surbiton - Kingston Tram	Mary Platford, NDD	From Talworth Hamlet to Tolworth Tower		with kind permission of the late Mary Platford
64	St. Matthew's Church Hall, now the cornerHOUSE Theatre		photograph taken for this book		kindly taken by Derek Winterburn
65	War Memorial, Ewell Road, unveiling, July 1920	Kingston photograph collection K2-0994	Kingston Museum and Heritage Service	local.history@rbk.kingston.gov.uk	
66	Election poster, 1918	Will Dyson poster for the Labour Party	Wikipedia Commons	https://commons.wikimedia.org/wiki	
68	Rev J C Banham	Framed photograph in St. Matthew's Church	St. Matthew's Parish Council		with kind permission of St. Matthew's PCC

page	Illustration	Origin	Publisher/Source	Web Site / Email	
69	Scout Troop	"A Point of View on Scouting"	St. Matthew's parish magazine		Reproduced by permission of Surrey History Centre
70	The Kingston by-pass - an early photograph	Kingston photograph collection K2-1588	Kingston Museum and Heritage Service	local.history@rbk.kingston.gov.uk	
71	David Lloyd George, circa 1920	press photograph purchased by the Library of Congress in 1948	Wikipedia Commons	https://commons.wikimedia.org/wiki	
72	Houses built in the 1920s in Cotterill Road		photograph taken for this book		kindly taken by Derek Winterburn
73	Advertisement for a Building Society. 1930s	Advertisement for Halifax Building Society mortgages	The Archives Hub	www.archiveshub.ac.uk	Courtesy of Lloyds Banking Group plc Archives

page	Illustration	Origin	Publisher/Source	Web Site / Email	
80	The school in Douglas Road		photograph taken for this book		kindly taken by Derek Winterburn
81	Original chapel of Our Lady Immaculate	Our Lady Immaculate web site	Our Lady Immaculate RC Church	www.olionline .co.uk	
82	St George's Church		photograph taken for this book		kindly taken by Derek Winterburn
84	Tolworth United Reformed Church	The Pastorate of Epsom, Ewell and Tolworth United Reformed Churches		http://epsom-ewell-tolworth.urc.org.uk	with kind permission of Tolworth United Reform Church
85	The Surbiton Lagoon opening	Kingston photograph collection	Kingston Museum and Heritage Service	local.history@rbk .kingston.gov.uk	

page	Illustration	Origin	Publisher/Source	Web Site / Email	
86	The Odeon Cinema, Tolworth, circa 1950	Photograph contributed by Ken Roe	Cinema Treasures	http://cinematreasures.org	
87	Mickey Mouse Club badge	List of avalable pinbacks from Disney	JB Beans	www.jbbeans.com	
89	"Air Raid Wardens Wanted" - 1939 poster	Photographed in Lincolnsfield Children's Centre, Bushey	"Join me in the 1900s"	www.1900s.org.uk	with kind permission of the Pat Cryer
90	Nash and Thompson gun turret (for Lancaster bomber)	Photographed by "Kogo"	Wikimedia	http://en.wikipedia.org/wiki/Nash_%26_Thomson	GNU Free Documentation License, Version 1.2
91	Berrylands Lawn Tennis Clubhouse	Surbiton Racket & Fitness Club		www.surbiton.org	with kind permission of Roy Staniland

page	Illustration	Origin	Publisher/Source	Web Site / Email	
92	Youth Fellowship - St. Matthew's and St. George's	Photograph from the collection of the late Brian Hawksbee	Hawksbee, 2013; YouByYou Books		with kind permission of Vivien Hawksbee
93	Our Lady Immaculate - the main church building	Our Lady Immaculate web site	Our Lady Immaculate RC Church	www.olionline.co.uk	
94	St. George's Church		photograph taken for this book		kindly taken by Derek Winterburn
96	The Toby Jug public house	The Toby Jug public house in 1965	The Francis Frith Collection	www.francisfrith.com	Copyright The Francis Frith Collection'
98	Motorcyclist, appx. 1955		Cafe Racer web site	www.caferacertv.com	

page	Illustration	Origin	Publisher/Source	Web Site / Email	
99	Surbiton Croquet Club - the Macrobertson Shield	Photograph from the collection of Surbiton Croquet Club	Surbiton Croquet Club		With kind permission of Bill Cannon
99	Alexandra Millennium Green - Anthony Trinkwon mowing				With kind permission of Anthony Trinkwon
100	Tolworth High Schools location		Google Earth		
101	The old Hollyfield School (now Kingston Councill Adult Education Center)		photograph taken for this book		taken by Bob Phillips
102	St. Matthews Parish School today - the new hall at the London International Studies Centre	From the LISC collection of photographs	LISC	http://londonisc.com	with kind permission of LISC Independent Tutorial College

page	Illustration	Origin	Publisher/Source	Web Site / Email
103	The Great London Council - its emblem		Wikipedia	https://en.wikipedia.org/wiki/Greater_London_Council
104	Tolworth Leisure Centre hosts a national karate competition	Press photo	GKR Karate (former site)	www.cix.co.uk
105	Tolworth Hospital		photograph taken for this book	taken by Bob Phillips
106	The South West London and St. George's Mental Health NHS Trust - new masters of Tolworth Hosptal	South West London and St. George's Mental Health NHS Trust		www.swlstg-tr.nhs.uk
107	The site of the Windsor Laundry		Google Earth	

page	Illustration	Origin	Publisher/Source	Web Site / Email	
108	The MoD / Toby Jug / Tesco's site - for development?		Google Earth		
109	The Gala Cosmetics Factory, Hook Rise	Kingston photograph collection K2-1395	Kingston Museum and Heritage Service	local.history@rbk .kingston.gov.uk	
110	The Tolworth Tower	Mary Platford, NDD	From Talworth Hamlet to Tolworth Tower		with kind permission of the late Mary Platford
112	54-76 The Broadway - a sample townscape		Google Maps Street View		
114	Proposed boundaries	Created in Powerpoint by the authors			

page	Illustration	Origin	Publisher/Source	Web Site / Email	
125	Broadway/Greenway - Tolworth, 2013	"Sherbet Dibdab" Article and photo in the Surrey Comet 16th August 2013	Gareth Harmer, photographer	www.deadlinepixltd .co.uk	with kind permission of Gareth Harmer and the Surrey Comet
128	Histogram documenting country of birth of Tolworth resodents 1971-2011	Created in Excel by the authors from census data	UK Data Service via the Kingston Data Observatory	http://census .ukdataservice.ac.uk	
133 ff	Proposed boundaries	Created in Powerpoint by the authors			
138	Tolworth Court position relative to the modern map	1895 OS map (see above), with annotations by the authors	Ordnance Survey		

page	Illustration	Origin	Publisher/Source	Web Site / Email
140	Map of Surbiton, 1855, showing southern boundary	Rowley Richardson's book Surbiton: 32 years of local self-government	Bull and Son, Victoria Road, Surbiton, 1888 (British Library)	
172	Tolworth's northern border, and the Alexandra recreational area		Google Earth	

With thanks to Bryon Dunn of Tolworth Photographic who digitally improved a number of the archive photographs used. The improved images are lodged in the Kingston Local History Centre Photographic Archive.

BIBLIOGRAPHY

Books refererred to in this volume

Joathanan Black, et al	The Picker House and Collection	PWP, 2013
John Blair	Medieval Surrey: Landholding, Church and Settlement Before 1300	1990, Sutton Publishing Ltd
Shaan Butters	That Famous Place: A History of Kingston upon Thames	2013, Kingston University Press
Edward W. Brayley et al	A Topographical History of Surrey, volume 2	J.S. Virtue & Co., 1850 and on
Mark Davison & Paul Adams	Tolworth Remembered	Mark Davison, 2000
Peter and Leni Gillman	Alias David Bowie	New English Library Ltd, 1987
G.B. Greenwood	Kingston upon Thames: A Dictionary of Local History	Martin & Greenwood, Walton
Alfred Heales	The Records of Merton Priory in the County of Surrey	Henry Frowde, London, 1898
Edna Healey	Coutts & Co: The Portrait of a Private Bank	Hodder & Stoughton, 1992
Richard F. Holmes	Pubs, Inns and Taverns of Surbiton and Malden	Wildhern Press, 2013

W Ravenhill	250 years of map making in the County of Surrey: A collection of reproductions of printed maps published between the years 1575-1823 with introductory notes	Phillimore & Co Ltd, 1974
Rowley W C Richardson	Surbiton, Thirty-two years of self-government	1888, reprinted British Library
June Sampson	All Change; Kingston, Surbiton and New Malden in the 19th Century	Marine Day, 1985
Patricia Ward	From Talworth Hamlet to Tolworth Tower: A History of the Tolworth Parish of St. Matthew's	1975

Contemporary Reference Books

Kelly's Directory (Kelly's, Post Office and Harrod & Co Directory)	Kelly's Directory Ltd.
Post Office Directory	HMG

Research/Journal/Newspaper articles

John Brown	The Coulthursts of Streatham Lodge	Local History Publications,
Kingston upon Thames Archaeological Society	Tolworth Court Farm dig report, 2000 www.pinan.co.uk/asoc/tolW00/tolworth.html	Kingston Museum and Heritage Service
Brian J Hawksbee	Tolworth – Population and Development, 1850-1900 (Diploma in Genealogy and History of the Family, University of London, 1990)	Kingston Museum and Heritage Service
Peter K Robins	Richard Jefferies at Tolworth	Kingston Museum and Heritage
June Sampson	A brush with the Pre-Raphaelites	Watford Observer, 28/11/1998
Royal Borough of Kingston upon Thames, Directorate of Education	Annual Report of Tolworth Recreation Centre, 1978-1979	Kingston Museum and Heritage Service
Heather Warne	Tolworth, Surrey: medieval settlement	Private communication, to be deposited in the National Archives, Arundel

Archival material referenced by the authors, with location		*reference*
National Archives, Kew	Sarjeants' Accounts, 1398-1401	SC6/1015/4-5
Surrey Local History Centre, Woking	Lands in the Manor of Talworth, 1820	QS6/4/29
National Archives , Arundel Castle	Records of Ewell Manor, 1461-85	M659, M647
Surrey Local History Centre, Woking	Manor of Tolworth; Book of Plans, 1803	Z/250
National Archives, East Sussex Record Office	Stewards' Memoranda Book (including Bounds and Perambulations), 1802-09	A5886/5
Surrey Local History Centre, Woking	Surveyors' Highway Book, 1841	2504

Bills and Acts of Government

The Tolworth Enclosure Act, 1820

The Local Government Act, 1894

Education Act of 1902

Web-sites used for reference

Samuel Williamson, Pres   MeasuringWorth.com   MeasuringWorth

Newspapers

                 Surrey Comet

                 St. Matthew's Parish Magazine

Other books consulted, but not specifically referenced by the authors

Charles Arnold Baker	The Companion to British History, 2nd edition	Routledge, 2001
Felipe Fernandez-Armesto	A History of England (in twelve volumes)	Folio Society, 1997–2002
Marion C Bone	The Story of 'Hook in Kingston'	St. Paul, Hook, 1989
Peter Brandon	A History of Surrey (Darwen County History)	Phillimore, 1998
G D H Cole and Raymond	The Common People	Methuen, 1938
Mark Davison	Surbiton Memories and more tales of old Tolworth and Berrylands	Mark Davison, 2004

Peter Fussell	Fish off the Slab: Progression through Long Ditton's long history	St. Mary, Long Ditton, 1994
Cecilia Hatt	History of Our Lady Immaculate, Tolworth	OLI Parish, 2008
Brian J Hawksbee	The Youth Fellowship of St Matthew's (Surbiton) and St George's (Tolworth): The story of youth work in a suburban Church of England parish from the 1940s to the 1960s	YouByYou Books, Biddenden, Kent, 2013
Alan A Jackson	Semi-Detached London: Suburban Development, Life and Transport, 1900-1939	Wild Swan Publications Ltd., 2nd ed., 1991 (1973)
John Morris	Domesday Book - Surrey	Phillimore, 1975
Edited by H E Malden	A History of the County of Surrey Volume 3 (Victoria History of the Counties of England)	Constable, 1902-1914
J W Molyneux-Child	The Evolution of the English Manorial System	Book Guild Ltd., 1987
Betty Owen	St. George's Church, Tolworth, 1934-1984	St. George's Church
Barbara C L Webb	Millais and the Hogsmill River: The Story of a Search to Find Where Sir John Millais Painted the Background of Ophelia, Complete with a Walk Retracing His Footsteps	Barbara Webb, 1997

ACKNOWLEDGEMENTS

In the production of this book "The Story of Tolworth", I am very aware of the help I have received from many people.

The work of the local Archive units are essential in the keeping of documents and in assisting the public working with them. I should particularly like to thank the workers at the centres in Kingston and in Surrey (Woking) where most of the sources relevant for this volume are kept. I should also like to thank the workers in the East Sussex archive in Brighton and the West Sussex archive in Arundel Castle.

Shaan Butters and Tim Everson, the pre-eminent historians of Kingston upon Thames, have been enormously generous with their time and expertise in reviewing a draft of this book and giving us most helpful input. Of course, the authors take entire responsibility for what is published here

I have also had advice from John Brown, concerning the Coulthurst family and the Streatham connection. As I am not a mediaevalist, I have been very dependent on Heather Warne, retired archivist of the National Archive, Arundel Castle and Dr Sandra Rayban of Cambridge University. The late Mary Platford produced the fine drawings for my earlier book "From Talworth Hamlet to Tolworth Tower" and we use them again in the current book, with her permission. Many of the new photographs taken for this book are the work of the Rev. Derek Winterburn. Brian Hawksbee has made an invaluable contribution both by his study of Victorian census returns and his book on the Youth Fellowship. I am grateful to Jeffrey Akerman for retrieving items for us from St. Matthew's and to Anna Cunnyngham for her poem, and for her support to the project.

Most of all I am grateful to my colleague Bob Phillips without whom this book would not have appeared. It was his idea that it should be undertaken. He has encouraged me, cajoled me and provided ideas. Bob wrote the Epilogue and the Appendices; he has edited the text and added to it, found the many illustrations and duocumented them and the bibliography.

Finally, I should like to thank my friends who have supported me and listen to my stories. I hope they enjoy reading the story of Tolworth as much as I have enjoyed writing it.

Pat Ward

INDEX